Wortschatz Oberstufe

Englisch-KOMPAKT

STARK

Autor: Rainer Jacob

Umschlagbild: © DrAfter123 / iStockphoto

© 2019 Stark Verlag GmbH
www.stark-verlag.de

Das Werk und alle seine Bestandteile sind urheberrechtlich geschützt.
Jede vollständige oder teilweise Vervielfältigung, Verbreitung und Veröffentlichung
bedarf der ausdrücklichen Genehmigung des Verlages. Dies gilt insbesondere für
Vervielfältigungen, Mikroverfilmungen sowie die Speicherung und Verarbeitung in
elektronischen Systemen.

Inhalt

Vorwort
Hinweise zu den digitalen Zusätzen
Abkürzungsverzeichnis

Human relations 1
1 Partnership 1
2 Family 2
3 Housekeeping 5
4 Feminist movement 7

Multicultural society 9
1 Immigration 9
2 Civil rights 16
3 Living in a diverse society 22

Crime 27
1 Crimes and offences 27
2 Drugs 31
3 The court/Law 33

Politics 41
1 Constitution/Political system 41
2 Executive/Government 43
3 Legislature/Parliament 48
4 Judiciary/Law 52
5 Elections 53

From Empire to the EU and Brexit 57
1 Empire 57
2 Commonwealth 61
3 European Union and Brexit 62

World affairs 69
1 War and peace 69
2 The world after 9/11 75
3 Ireland – The Troubles 80

Economy 85
1. Economic policy and business economics 85
2. Managing finances 90
3. Consumer 95
4. Advertising 99

The world of work 103
1. Working life 103
2. Work-life balance, diversity and compliance 109
3. Trade unions 113

Agriculture and developing countries 115
1. Agriculture 115
2. Problems in developing countries 118

Environment 123
1. The world around us 123
2. Air pollution 126
3. Water pollution 129
4. Waste 130
5. Energy 131

Science and technology 133
1. Genetic engineering 133
2. Computers and digital technology 142

Media 147
1. Television, radio and streaming services 147
2. Newspapers, magazines and (e-)books 150
3. Social media 155

Britisches und amerikanisches Englisch 157

False friends 161

Grundwortschatz 165

Autor: Rainer Jacob

Vorwort

Liebe Schülerin, lieber Schüler,

Vokabeln sind das A und O einer Sprache. In allen Bereichen des Englischunterrichts – um Texte zu verstehen, Fragen zu beantworten, Meinungen differenziert auszudrücken, eine Sprachmittlung anzufertigen – sind gute Wortschatzkenntnisse unerlässlich.

Mit diesem Band aus der Reihe „Englisch-KOMPAKT" können Sie Ihren aktiven und passiven Wortschatz erweitern und festigen. Die für Prüfungen und Klausuren wichtigsten Vokabeln sind in übersichtlichen Wort- und Sachfeldern nach den Themenbereichen der Englischlehrpläne zusammengestellt. Zusätzlich zum gedruckten Buch stehen Ihnen alle Vokabeln auch als digitale Lernkarten in der Web-App „MindCards" zur Verfügung. Die App enthält auch Hörbeispiele, mit denen Sie sich die richtige Aussprache anhören können. Nähere Informationen hierzu finden Sie unter „Hinweise zu den digitalen Zusätzen".

Außer der deutschen Bedeutung eines Wortes ist jeweils auch ein einprägsamer Beispielsatz oder eine Definition angegeben. Das erleichtert das Lernen und Behalten des Wortschatzes und macht feine Bedeutungsunterschiede erkennbar, sodass die Vokabeln in entsprechenden Sprech- und Schreibsituationen selbstständig angewendet werden können. Angaben von Synonymen und Antonymen fördern die Erweiterung des Wortschatzes.

Zum schnellen Nachschlagen und zur Orientierung steht ein umfangreicher Anhang zur Verfügung:
- eine Zusammenstellung von Begriffen, für die im britischen bzw. amerikanischen Englisch unterschiedliche Wörter verwendet werden (z. B. „bill" [BE] und „check" [AE] für Rechnung)
- eine Liste der sogenannten „falschen Freunde", die oft zu Fehlern verleiten („sensible" heißt nicht „sensibel")
- ein Verzeichnis von Vokabeln des Grundwortschatzes mit Übersetzung.

Für die Erweiterung Ihres Wortschatzes und die Vorbereitung auf Ihre Prüfungen wünsche ich Ihnen viel Erfolg.

Rainer Jacob

Hinweise zu den digitalen Zusätzen

MindCards – digitale Lernkarten mit Hörbeispielen

Die Vokabeln aus diesem Band stehen Ihnen auch als digitale Lernkarten in der Web-App **MindCards** zur Verfügung. Sie können sie online mit Ihrem Smartphone abrufen und haben so Ihren mobilen Karteikasten überall mit dabei. Hörbeispiele helfen Ihnen bei der richtigen Aussprache der Vokabeln.

Die MindCards können direkt im Browser geöffnet werden, die Installation über einen App-Store ist nicht erforderlich. Scannen Sie einfach den nebenstehenden QR-Code mit dem Smartphone oder geben Sie den folgenden Link ein:
https://www.stark-verlag.de/mindcards/90462d

Und so arbeiten Sie mit den MindCards:
- Wählen Sie eines oder mehrere (Teil-)Kapitel aus, die Sie bearbeiten möchten.
- Tippen Sie dann auf „alle Karten laden", um die Bearbeitung zu starten.
- Über den Audio-Button auf den Lernkarten können Sie sich die richtige Aussprache der englischen Begriffe anhören.
- Durch Tippen auf den Screen können Sie die Karte umdrehen, um sich die Übersetzung anzeigen zu lassen.
- Entscheiden Sie bei jeder Vokabel, ob Sie sie schon sicher beherrschen oder noch nicht gewusst hätten.
- Am Ende des Kapitels oder wenn Sie die Bearbeitung abbrechen, erhalten Sie eine Auswertung.
- Die Vokabelkarten werden dann in verschiedenen „Stapeln" abgelegt, sodass Sie z. B. alle Wörter, die Sie noch nicht gewusst haben, noch einmal gesondert wiederholen können.

Video „Strategien zum Vokabellernen"

Über den folgenden QR-Code oder Link können Sie sich ein Video mit vielen nützlichen Tipps zum Vokabellernen ansehen:
https://www.stark-verlag.de/video/90462d

Im Hinblick auf eine eventuelle Begrenzung des Datenvolumens wird empfohlen, dass Sie sich bei der Nutzung der digitalen Zusätze im WLAN befinden.

Abkürzungsverzeichnis

AE	American English
BE	British English
e. g.	lat. exempli gratia = for example
esp.	especially
etw.	etwas
GB	Great Britain
i. e.	lat. id est = das heißt
jdm.	jemandem
jdn.	jemanden
Pl.	Plural
sb	somebody
Sg.	Singular
sl.	Slang
sth	something
UK	United Kingdom, *hier:* Begriff ist nur in Großbritannien relevant
US	United States, *hier:* Begriff ist nur in den USA relevant
≠	Antonym
=	Synonym

Human relations

1 Partnership

vocabulary	dt. Bedeutung	English phrase	syn/opp
(to) become engaged	sich verloben	Mary has become engaged to John.	
cohabitation	Zusammenleben ohne Trauschein	Cohabitation has become more widespread.	
divorce	Scheidung	Britain has a high divorce rate.	≠ marriage
domestic violence	Gewalt in der Ehe, häusliche Gewalt	Unfortunately, incidents of domestic violence are on the increase.	
engaged	verlobt	having agreed to marry sb	
engagement	Verlobung	an agreement to marry	
marital status	Familienstand	My marital status is "single".	= civil status
marriage	Heirat, Ehe	They can look back on 25 years of marriage.	≠ divorce
(to) marry	heiraten	He would only marry for love, not for money.	≠ to divorce
mixed marriage	„Mischehe"	a marriage in which partners belong to different races	
(to) propose	einen Heiratsantrag machen	He was afraid that if he proposed she might refuse.	
same-sex marriage	gleichgeschlechtliche Ehe	Legislation to allow same-sex marriage in England was passed in 2013.	= gay marriage
single	ledig	Many people remain single today.	≠ married

2 Human relations

vocabulary	dt. Bedeutung	English phrase	syn/opp
women's shelter	Frauenhaus	a place for women who have become victims of domestic violence	= women's centre

2 Family

vocabulary	dt. Bedeutung	English phrase	syn/opp
abortion	Abtreibung	Most abortions take place before 12 weeks of pregnancy.	≠ fertilisation
(to) adopt a child	ein Kind adoptieren	Couples who cannot have children of their own often wish to adopt a child.	
adoption	Adoption	The young parents gave up their baby daughter for adoption.	
(to) bear a child	ein Kind gebären	to give birth to a child	
birth-control	Geburtenkontrolle, Verhütung	Without proper birth-control there will be many more mouths to feed.	
(to) bring up children	Kinder erziehen, aufziehen	My grandmother brought up five children.	= to rear, to raise
(to) care for children	Kinder betreuen	Caring for children is a fulltime job.	
child abuse	Kindesmisshandlung	A recent TV documentary about child abuse made viewers aware of the problem.	= ill-treatment, mal-treatment, neglect
child allowance	Kindergeld	A legitimate or illegitimate child, stepchild or adopted child is entitled to child allowance.	= children's allowance
child care	Kinderbetreuung	Firms are improving child care facilities.	

Human relations 3

vocabulary	dt. Bedeutung	English phrase	syn/opp
child minder	*Tagesmutter, Kinderbetreuer*in*	Many working parents cannot afford a child minder.	= babysitter
child molestation	*Kindesmissbrauch*	An American superstar was accused of child molestation.	
childbirth	*Entbindung*	His wife died in childbirth.	
(to) conceive a child conception	*ein Kind empfangen Empfängnis*	She conceived her first child at 17.	
contraception	*(Empfängnis-) Verhütung*	the practice and methods of preventing a woman from becoming pregnant	
delivery	*Entbindung*	Her delivery was easier than expected.	
delivery room	*Kreißsaal*	She was taken to the delivery room straight away.	
expectant mother	*werdende Mutter*	a pregnant woman	
family allowance	*Kinder-/Familienbeihilfe*	amount of money that is given to a mother/father	
foster child	*Pflegekind*	a child who is taken care of by a couple who are not his/her legal parents	
(to) give birth to a child	*ein Kind gebären*	Sarah gave birth to her second child at 35.	= to bear a child
(to) have a baby	*ein Kind bekommen*	Women are deciding to have babies later in life.	
illegitimate child	*uneheliches Kind*	a child born to parents who are not married to each other	≠ legitimate child
maternity	*Mutterschaft*	The government has doubled the maternity grant.	= motherhood

Human relations

vocabulary	dt. Bedeutung	English phrase	syn/opp
maternity leave	*Mutterschutz*	An expectant mother is entitled to take maternity leave before and after the birth of her child.	
only child	*Einzelkind*	An only child does not have any brothers or sisters.	
parental leave	*Elternzeit*	Raymond took parental leave when his son David was born.	= family leave
patchwork family	*Familie, in der Kinder von verschiedenen Eltern aufwachsen*	The number of patchwork families is on the increase.	
pregnancy	*Schwangerschaft*	Contraception helps prevent an unplanned pregnancy.	
pregnancy test	*Schwangerschaftstest*	A pregnancy test can be carried out within a few days after conception.	
pregnant	*schwanger*	Mrs Miller is pregnant with her fourth child.	
problem child	*Sorgenkind*	Doris Lessing's novel *The Fifth Child* is about how a family copes with a problem child.	
same-sex parented family	*Regenbogenfamilie (Familie, bei der die Elternteile gleichgeschlechtlich sind)*	Jonah grows up in a same-sex parented family – he has got two mums.	= LGBT family
single mother/father	*allein erziehende*r Mutter/ Vater*	Tom is a single father of two and works full time.	= single parent

Human relations 5

vocabulary	dt. Bedeutung	English phrase	syn/opp
skip-generation family	Familie, in der die Kinder von den Großeltern erzogen werden	a family in which children are raised by their grandparents	
(to) start a family	eine Familie gründen	Jennifer and Henry started a family when they were still teenagers.	
stepmother/ stepfather	Stiefmutter/ Stiefvater	Cinderella is mistreated by her stepmother and elder sisters.	
(to) support a family	eine Familie ernähren	Jeremy and Amy, who still go to school, don't earn any money and therefore cannot support a family.	= to sustain a family
surrogate mother surrogate motherhood	Leihmutter Leihmutterschaft	Some couples who cannot have children seek the help of a surrogate mother to bear their child.	

3 Housekeeping

vocabulary	dt. Bedeutung	English phrase	syn/opp
breadwinner	Hauptverdiener*in	Not every husband is prepared to give up his role as breadwinner.	= wage earner
chores	(lästige) Hausarbeit	I hate doing chores.	= household tasks
(to) confine	darauf beschränken	Women in conservative countries are often confined to their traditional roles as wives, mothers, and homemakers.	= to restrict, to limit
convenience food	Fertiggericht	Do you prefer home-cooked meals or convenience foods?	

Human relations

vocabulary	dt. Bedeutung	English phrase	syn/opp
(to) do housework	Hausarbeit machen	After returning from the office I have to do some housework.	
(to) do the housekeeping	sich um den Haushalt kümmern	taking care of a house	
domestic	Haus-	connected with the home or family	
domestic help	Haushaltshilfe	Many American families employ undocumented immigrants as domestic helps.	
domestic science	Hauswirtschaftskunde	Jamie O'Connor always earned top marks in domestic science.	
household appliances	Haushaltsgeräte	Household appliances have freed us from labour-intensive chores.	= household devices, gadgets
housekeeping money	Haushaltsgeld	the money used to buy food, cleaning materials etc.	
labour-intensive	arbeitsintensiv	Many labour-intensive chores have been associated with housework.	
monotonous	eintönig	never changing	≠ varied
repetitive	sich ständig wiederholend	Machines like dishwashers have freed us from repetitive jobs in the house.	= tedious, boring, dull

4 Feminist movement

vocabulary	dt. Bedeutung	English phrase	syn/opp
emancipation	Emanzipation	For centuries women have fought for their rights and emancipation.	= liberation
equal pay	gleiche Bezahlung	Women are entitled to equal pay with men when they are doing the same work.	
equality	Gleichheit	the same status for all members of a society	
feminist movement	Frauenrechtsbewegung	The feminist movement has profoundly changed women's lives.	= feminism, women's movement
woman suffrage	Wahlrecht für Frauen	Woman suffrage was achieved in the first half of the 20th century in many countries.	= women's suffrage
women's liberation movement/ women's lib	Frauenrechtsbewegung	The women's liberation movement seeks equal rights for women.	

Multicultural society

1 Immigration

vocabulary	dt. Bedeutung	English phrase	syn/opp
abode right of abode	Aufenthalt Wohn-, Aufenthaltsrecht	In 1971 Commonwealth citizens lost their right of abode in the UK.	
(to) accelerate	beschleunigen	The immigrants accelerated the economic growth of the country.	= to quicken, to speed, to facilitate
(to) advance	voranbringen, fördern	to bring or move forward, to raise to a higher rank	= to promote ≠ to hold back
advanced	fortschrittlich	A number of immigrants came from countries with advanced political and economic institutions.	= progressive
adverse	widrig, feindlich, ungünstig, nachteilig	The settlers had to cope with adverse weather conditions.	= hostile, unfavourable, bad ≠ favourable
alien	Ausländer*in, Fremde*r	a person of another race or nation or born in a foreign country	= foreigner, stranger
(to) alienate	entfremden	to make sb feel isolated	
ancestor	Vorfahr*in	a person or a member of the family living in an earlier generation	= forebear ≠ descendant
ancestry	Abstammung	Some people use DNA tests to find out about their ancestry.	
approximately	ungefähr	Between 1815 and 1860 approximately five million people emigrated to America.	= about, roughly

Multicultural society

vocabulary	dt. Bedeutung	English phrase	syn/opp
(to) argue	sich für etw. aussprechen	The senator argued for a different immigration policy.	= to call for, to support
aspiration	Bestrebung, Hoffnung, Ehrgeiz	sb's hope to achieve sth	= ambition
(to) assimilate	(sich) anpassen, (sich) eingliedern	It is sometimes very hard for newcomers to assimilate into the new society.	
asylum	Asyl	the protection granted by a state, for example to a political refugee	
asylum seeker	Asylsuchende*r	sb looking for protection abroad	
citizen	Staatsbürger*in	In 1971 Commonwealth citizens lost their right of abode in the UK.	
citizenship	Staatsbürgerschaft	Immigrants can apply for citizenship after five years.	
conviction (to) convince	Überzeugung überzeugen	Analysts expressed their conviction that immigrants contribute to the productivity of a country.	
deportation (to) deport	Ausweisung, Abschiebung abschieben	The deportation of illegal immigrants has been made easier.	
descendant	Nachkomme, Nachfahr*in	a person or a family member living in a later generation	≠ ancestor
desperate	verzweifelt	being in a bad or frightening situation	
(to) detain	festhalten, warten lassen	The illegal immigrants were detained by the police for 24 hours.	
(to) diminish	sich verringern, abnehmen	The Native American population diminished rapidly as white settlement advanced.	= to decrease

Multicultural society

vocabulary	dt. Bedeutung	English phrase	syn/opp
Ellis Island	*Ellis Island*	From 1892 until 1943 Ellis Island served as the main entry point for immigrants by sea to the US.	
(to) emigrate	*auswandern*	to leave one's country	
entry procedure	*Einreise-, Aufnahmeverfahren*	Entry procedures at Ellis Island were frightening for many newcomers.	
(to) estimate	*(ab-)schätzen*	Experts estimate that the number of immigrants will increase.	
ferry boat	*Fährschiff, Fähre*	a (small) ship to transport people over a short distance	
flight **(to) flee**	*Flucht* *fliehen, flüchten*	the act of escaping	
founding fathers	*Gründerväter*	The founding fathers of the United States were the members of the American Constitutional Convention of 1787.	
freedom of worship	*Religionsfreiheit, freie Religionsausübung*	From the days of the Pilgrims people have come to America in search of freedom of worship.	
frontier	*Grenze, Grenzgebiet*	the line or area separating two countries US: borderline between civilisation and wilderness	= border
gateway	*Tor*	Ellis Island was the gateway to the US.	
green card	*Aufenthaltserlaubnis*	a permit allowing a foreign national to live and work permanently in the US	

Multicultural society

vocabulary	dt. Bedeutung	English phrase	syn/opp
homeland	*Heimatland*	Many Jamaicans left their homeland because they couldn't find any work.	= native country
immigrant	*Einwanderer/ Einwanderin*	Numerous immigrants came to the USA in search of liberty.	≠ emigrant
immigration act	*Einwanderungs- gesetz*	An immigration act was passed to reduce the number of people who wanted to live and work in the UK.	= bill, law
immigration quota	*Einwanderungs- quote*	From 1924 to 1968 immigration to the US was regulated according to an immigration quota system.	
indignation	*Entrüstung*	angry criticism, often expressed because of unfair treatment	
ineligible	*nicht berechtigt, ungeeignet*	Political activists were declared ineligible for immigration.	= unsuitable, unfit
influx	*Zustrom*	Many British politicians tried to stop the influx of people from Commonwealth countries.	= inflow
interpreter	*Dolmetscher*in*	Most immigrants needed the help of an interpreter to understand the questions of the immigration officers.	
(to) intimidate	*einschüchtern*	Sweatshop employers often intimidated their illegal workers.	= to scare, to frighten
(to) invigorate	*stärken*	The contributions of the immigrants invigorated the nation's life.	= to strengthen, to reinforce, to intensify

Multicultural society

vocabulary	dt. Bedeutung	English phrase	syn/opp
landmark	Wahrzeichen	The Statue of Liberty is one of New York's famous landmarks.	
(to) line up	sich anstellen	to stand and wait in a queue	
low-status job	Arbeit mit geringem Ansehen, niedere Arbeit	When immigrants first arrived they often had to accept low-status jobs.	
(to) lure	anlocken	Adventurers were lured to the US because of the open unexplored wilderness of the country.	
melting pot	Schmelztiegel	Americans have always believed that their country was a melting pot of nations.	
migrant worker	Wanderarbeiter*in, Gastarbeiter*in	a worker who travels to wherever he/she can find work	
migration (to) migrate	(Völker-)Wanderung, Migration (ab-, aus-)wandern	Sociologists study migration to analyse the effects it has on the social structure.	
native	einheimisch	The Maori are the native population of New Zealand.	= indigenous
native language	Muttersprache	A lot of Hispanic immigrants want to preserve their native language and speak Spanish to their children.	= mother tongue
(to) naturalise naturalisation	einbürgern Einbürgerung	to give a foreigner the citizenship of a country	
newcomer	Neuankömmling	a person who has recently arrived	

Multicultural society

vocabulary	dt. Bedeutung	English phrase	syn/opp
nightmare	*Albtraum*	an unpleasant and terrible dream	
ordeal	*schwere Prüfung, Qual, Tortur*	For many immigrants the examinations at Ellis Island were an ordeal.	
outlaw	*Geächtete*r, Bandit*in*	a person who has broken the law	
penniless	*mittellos, ohne Geld*	Illegal and undocumented immigrants from Mexico arrived in the States completely penniless.	
(to) persecute	*verfolgen*	Racists persecute a minority out of prejudice, hatred or envy.	
pledge	*Versprechen, Gelöbnis*	a formal promise	
prejudiced	*voreingenommen*	Some older immigrants were prejudiced against the newcomers from Eastern Europe.	= biased
prospect	*Aussicht*	The immigrant had the prospect of earning a living for herself and her family.	= chance, expectation, hope
(to) provide	*zur Verfügung stellen*	Some migrants have their own businesses and provide employment.	= to give, to offer
refuge	*Zuflucht*	a safe place which protects from danger or trouble	= shelter
refugee	*Flüchtling, Geflüchtete*r*	a person who has had to leave his/her country or home, because of a war or for political or religious reasons	
relative	*Verwandte*r*	a member of one's family	

Multicultural society

vocabulary	dt. Bedeutung	English phrase	syn/opp
(to) relocate	*umsiedeln*	Young immigrant families were willing to pack their belongings and relocate to another part of the continent.	= to move
resentment	*Abneigung, Groll, Missgunst*	Discrimination and resentment between ethnic groups are often still alive below the surface.	= ill-feeling, jealousy, grudge
reservation	*Vorbehalt*	Some of the immigrants were met with reservation.	
resettlement	*Umsiedlung*	The European Commission started a new resettlement programme for people seeking protection.	= relocation
residence permit	*Aufenthaltserlaubnis*	When they first arrive, refugees are given a residence permit for a limited time period.	
restriction	*Ein-, Beschränkung*	Canada introduced severe restrictions on the number of immigrants.	
riches [Pl.]	*Reichtum, Reichtümer*	The search of riches and prosperity has brought millions to America.	= wealth
salad bowl	*Salatschüssel*	metaphor for people of different races and cultural backgrounds living together in a nation	
(to) seek	*suchen*	Not all immigrants found what they sought.	
shelter	*Unterkunft*	a place giving protection from bad weather or danger	

Multicultural society

vocabulary	dt. Bedeutung	English phrase	syn/opp
(to) slow down	verringern, verlangsamen	The Immigration Bill of 1971 was passed to slow down the influx of people from Commonwealth nations.	
sweatshop	Ausbeutungsbetrieb	a small factory in which people work in very bad conditions	
tide	Flut, Zustrom	In the 19th century a tide of immigration began bringing more than 40,000,000 persons into the country up to 1960.	= inflow, influx
undocumented	ohne (Ausweis-) Papiere	Employers in the sweatshops of the textile industry exploited many undocumented immigrants.	= non-registered, illegal
xenophobia	Ausländerfeindlichkeit	Unfortunately, xenophobia has always existed.	
yearning	Sehnsucht	a strong and urgent desire	

2 Civil rights

vocabulary	dt. Bedeutung	English phrase	syn/opp
(to) adhere to adherence	festhalten an, befolgen Einhaltung	Employers should adhere to civil rights laws.	
(to) affect	sich auswirken	to produce an effect on sb or sth	
(to) affirm	versichern, bekräftigen	to state as a fact	

Multicultural society

vocabulary	dt. Bedeutung	English phrase	syn/opp
affirmative action	*Förderungsmaßnahme zugunsten von Minderheiten*	efforts to increase the educational or employment opportunities of socially disadvantaged groups	
(to) amend	*ändern, ergänzen*	The Voting Rights Act of 1965 was last amended in 1992.	
(to) assassinate	*ermorden*	Martin Luther King was assassinated in Memphis in 1968.	= to kill, to murder
(to) assist assistance	*helfen, unterstützen* *Unterstützung*	The department assists in the elimination of discrimination.	= to help, to support
attempt	*Versuch*	The new legislation is an attempt to bring about social justice.	
(to be) barred from	*ausgeschlossen (sein) von*	Many African Americans are still barred from equal opportunities at work.	= (to be) excluded from
basis	*Grundlage*	It is illegal to discriminate on the basis of race, sex or religion.	
civil rights	*Bürgerrechte*	African Americans had been denied civil rights (for example the right to vote) for too long.	
civil rights movement	*Bürgerrechtsbewegung*	The Civil Rights Movement of the 1960s was led by Martin Luther King.	
clause	*Klausel, Bestimmung*	The equal protection clause of the 14th Amendment (1868) provides that "all persons born or naturalized in the United States … are citizens of the United States."	

Multicultural society

vocabulary	dt. Bedeutung	English phrase	syn/opp
complaint	Beschwerde, Klage	a statement that a product or a situation is unsatisfactory or unacceptable	
conciliation	Versöhnung, Besänftigung	A conciliation committee was set up to settle disputes between the different groups.	
(to) consult	um Rat fragen; sich beraten	The members of the Amnesty groups consult each other on new projects.	= to ask sb for advice
creed	Überzeugung, Weltanschauung	We believe in equal rights for all citizens regardless of race, colour, creed or sexual orientation.	= belief
(to) defend	verteidigen	A newly elected US president swears to defend the Constitution of the United States.	
degradation	Erniedrigung	In the court case the two women complained about the degradation of sexual harassment.	
(to) deny	verweigern, leugnen	African Americans have long been denied equal rights.	
denial	Verweigerung, Ablehnung		
(to) deprive	jdm. etw. nehmen	African Americans were deprived of their civil rights for a long time.	≠ to grant
deprivation	Entbehrung		
despair	Verzweiflung	Martin Luther King was never in despair about the just cause of his fight.	
disability	Behinderung	The new law improved the situation of people with one or more physical or mental disabilities.	= challenge

Multicultural society

vocabulary	dt. Bedeutung	English phrase	syn/opp
discrimination	*unterschiedliche Behandlung, Benachteiligung*	Discrimination on the basis of race, colour or national origin is against the law.	
disparity	*Ungleichheit*	a great difference	≠ sameness, likeness, parity
(to) endure	*ertragen*	to bear an unpleasant situation	= to suffer, to tolerate
(to) enforce	*durchsetzen*	to put sth into effect or operation	= to effect, to implement
enforcement	*Durchsetzung (eines Rechts oder Gesetzes)*	The Equal Opportunities Commission sees to the enforcement of the Equal Pay Act.	
enslavement	*Versklavung*	to make sb a slave	
equal opportunities	*Chancengleichheit*	Everyone should enjoy equal opportunities.	
(to) expand	*erweitern, ausdehnen*	In 2015 the Supreme Court expanded the law to include same-sex marriage.	
(to) file a lawsuit	*eine Klage einreichen*	Martin Luther King and his supporters filed a lawsuit against the city council of Montgomery.	
(to) forbid	*verbieten*	to refuse to allow sth	= to prohibit, to ban ≠ to permit, to allow
gender	*Geschlecht*	In 1928, Britain introduced the general right of voting; it ended all discrimination according to one's gender or social rank.	sex: often used to refer to biological differences; gender: refers to cultural or social ones

vocabulary	dt. Bedeutung	English phrase	syn/opp
guidance	*Beratung*	giving sb advice or information on how to solve a problem	
(to) humiliate	*demütigen, erniedrigen*	to make sb feel ashamed	
inferiority	*Minderwertigkeit*	the feeling of not being as good as others	
liberation	*Befreiung*	Civil rights activists fight for the liberation of oppressed people everywhere.	= freeing
moderate	*maßvoll, gemäßigt*	Martin Luther King's moderate views were not shared by all black leaders.	= reasonable ≠ extreme
non-violent	*gewaltlos*	M. L. King adopted the means of non-violent protest from Mahatma Gandhi.	
(to) oppress **oppression**	*unterdrücken* *Unterdrückung*	Unfortunately, ethnic, religious and sexual minorities are still oppressed in many countries.	= to suppress, to persecute
prejudice	*Vorurteil*	an unfair judgment of a person or a group of people, often caused by a lack of information	
race relations	*Beziehungen zwischen Menschen unterschiedlicher ethnischer Herkunft*	Do you think race relations have improved over the past few years?	
(to) register	*in das Wählerverzeichnis eintragen*	to enrol sb as a voter	

Multicultural society

vocabulary	dt. Bedeutung	English phrase	syn/opp
(to) require	*verlangen, vorschreiben*	In all Montgomery buses, black passengers were required to sit at the back.	
requirement	*Bedingung, Voraussetzung*		
retaliation	*Vergeltung(s-maßnahme)*	Martin Luther King rejected all acts of revenge and retaliation.	
(to) retaliate	*sich rächen*		
right to vote	*Stimmrecht*	African Americans were denied the right to vote for too long.	= suffrage, franchise
segregation	*Abtrennung, Absonderung, (Rassen-)Trennung*	In 1954, the Supreme Court decided that racial segregation in schools was against the Constitution.	
statute	*Gesetz, Statut*	a written law which was passed by parliament	= law
unalienable	*unveräußerlich*	The US Declaration of Independence guarantees the people's unalienable rights.	
unconstitutional	*verfassungswidrig*	The US Supreme Court ruled that racial segregation in public transportation was unconstitutional.	
unlawful	*rechtswidrig*	against the law	
violation	*Verletzung*	Hate crimes are a violation of civil rights.	= offence
(to) violate	*verletzen*		
void	*nichtig*	The Supreme Court declares acts of Congress which violate the country's basic laws as null and void.	= invalid

3 Living in a diverse society

vocabulary	dt. Bedeutung	English phrase	syn/opp
(to) adapt	*(sich) anpassen*	Young people often adapt more quickly to new surroundings than older generations.	
(to) appal	*entsetzen, schockieren*	Incidents of racist police violence have appalled the public.	= to shock
(to) appreciate	*wertschätzen*	People don't always appreciate the advantages of diversity.	
attitude	*Haltung, Einstellung*	The prime minister warned that anti-immigrant attitudes could intensify.	= feeling, sentiment, view
belonging	*Zugehörigkeit*	Refugees must be given a chance to develop a sense of belonging.	
bias	*Vorurteil, Voreingenommenheit*	A new programme was introduced to counteract bias against minorities.	= prejudice
civil courage	*Zivilcourage*	To stand up against racist behaviour is a sign of civil courage.	= moral courage
clash	*Zusammenstoß*	There were violent clashes between protesters and counterprotesters.	
(to) contribute contribution	*beitragen Beitrag*	In the long run, immigrants will contribute to a country's wealth.	
disadvantaged	*benachteiligt*	The policy of affirmative action was meant to improve the chances of people from disadvantaged groups.	

Multicultural society

vocabulary	dt. Bedeutung	English phrase	syn/opp
disconcerting	beunruhigend	The rising number of hate crimes is disconcerting.	
dispossessed	Besitzlose, Enteignete	people who don't own anything	
distinct	verschieden, deutlich	New York City alone has more than 170 distinct ethnic communities.	= different
diverse	verschiedenartig, gemischt	The US is a culturally diverse country.	= mixed, varied
diversity	Vielfalt	Cultural diversity is one of the main characteristics of a multi-ethnic society.	= variety
(to) embrace	(bereitwillig) aufgreifen, annehmen	We should learn to embrace diversity.	
empowerment	Empowerment, Stärkung	Our company promotes the goals of gender equality and empowerment of women.	
encounter	Begegnung	Encounters with people from diverse backgrounds can be very enriching.	
ethnic	Volks-	There are many different ethnic groups in the USA.	
grudge	Groll, Neid	Holding a grudge against someone is not healthy – you should learn to let it go.	= resentment
handicap	Behinderung	Discrimination on the basis of race, sex, handicap and national origin is illegal.	= disability
homeless people	Obdachlose	people without a roof over their heads	

Multicultural society

vocabulary	dt. Bedeutung	English phrase	syn/opp
(to) identify with	sich identifizieren mit	Some young Muslims find it hard to identify with the traditional Islam practised at home by their families.	
inclusion	Inklusion, Einbeziehung	Inclusion means, for example, that people with disabilities have the same possibilities to participate in society as non-disabled people.	
marginalised group	gesellschaftliche Randgruppe	Homeless teenagers have been a marginalised group in society for too long.	
minority	Minderheit	The United Kingdom has a large Asian minority.	≠ majority
misfit	Außenseiter*in	a person who is different from the masses and does not fit into society	= outsider
multi-racial	gemischtrassig	The US is a multi-racial society.	
neighbourly help	Nachbarschaftshilfe	A new social club was set up to provide neighbourly help for older people.	
pluralistic society	pluralistische Gesellschaft	The United States is not homogeneous; it is a pluralistic society.	
(to) populate	bevölkern	Brixton, a district in South London, is populated by black people, e. g. from the West Indies.	
(to be) prejudiced against	voreingenommen (sein) gegen	Too many people are still prejudiced against foreigners.	= (to be) biased against

vocabulary	dt. Bedeutung	English phrase	syn/opp
pursuit	Streben, Verfolgung, Trachten	Among the basic human rights are: life, liberty and the pursuit of happiness.	
resistance (to) resist	Widerstand widerstehen, standhalten	Resistance to teaching children in English and Spanish has increased in California.	= opposition
social commitment	soziales Engagement	The mayor praised the volunteers for their social commitment.	= civic engagement
(to) tackle	fertig werden mit, (ein Problem) anpacken	It is essential to tackle the problems of homelessness and poverty.	= to cope with, to manage
tension	Spannung	Differences of opinion should not lead to social tensions.	
tolerance	Toleranz	Tolerance is one of the most important values in society.	
underprivileged	schlechtergestellt, unterprivilegiert	Underprivileged children must get access to education, proper healthcare etc.	= deprived, disadvantaged
volunteering	Ehrenamt, ehrenamtliche Arbeit	Rita's hobbies include volunteering with social action groups.	
welcoming culture	Willkommenskultur	Some countries have developed a new welcoming culture and support refugees.	

Crime

1 Crimes and offences

vocabulary	dt. Bedeutung	English phrase	syn/opp
abuse (to) abuse	*Missbrauch missbrauchen*	wrong or bad treatment	= mistreatment
armed robbery	*bewaffneter Raub*	using weapons to commit a robbery	
arson	*Brandstiftung*	the deliberate criminal act of setting fire to a building	
(to) beat up	*verprügeln*	Supporters of the visiting football team were beaten up by hooligans.	
(to) betray	*verraten*	Jesus was betrayed by Judas.	
bloodshed	*Blutvergießen*	The crusades caused massive bloodshed.	
bribery	*Bestechung*	accepting money in return for a favour	= corruption
burglary	*Einbruch, Einbruchdiebstahl*	entering a building illegally and stealing things from it	
CCTV (closed circuit television)	*Videoüberwachung*	a system of cameras used in many public places or buildings to protect them from crime	
(to) cheat	*betrügen*	to act in a dishonest or unfair way in order to get an advantage for yourself	= to deceive, to trick, to swindle
child abuse	*Kindesmissbrauch*	Child abuse is a most disgusting crime.	
conspiracy	*Verschwörung*	a secret plan, e. g. to overthrow the government	= plot

Crime

vocabulary	dt. Bedeutung	English phrase	syn/opp
convict	Verurteilte*r, Sträfling	Towards the end of the 18th century convicts were shipped to Australia as a punishment.	= criminal, offender, prisoner
(to) convict	überführen, verurteilen		
crime rate	Kriminalitätsrate	number of unlawful acts within a certain period of time	
crime-ridden	von Verbrechen heimgesucht	Most tourists avoid the run-down and crime-ridden areas of big cities.	
cyberbullying	Internetschikane, Cybermobbing	Cyberbullying has become a widespread problem.	= cyberabuse
cybercrime	Internetkriminalität	Cybercrime is increasing.	= computer crime
cyberstalking	Cyberstalking (Belästigung über das Internet)	The officers who investigate cases of cyberstalking made several arrests.	
delinquency	Kriminalität	bad or criminal behaviour	
detention centre	Erziehungsanstalt	an institution for reforming and training young offenders	= borstal [UK]
deviance	Abweichung	strange and morally unacceptable behaviour	
(to) exact	(dringend) fordern, eintreiben	to demand (sometimes using force or threats)	
felony	Schwerverbrechen	a serious crime	
(to) fiddle [sl.]	manipulieren, betrügen	The accountant fiddled the books of the company.	= to cheat, to con, to swindle
(to) forge forgery	fälschen Fälschung	to make a copy of sth in order to deceive people	= to falsify, to counterfeit
fraud	Betrug	The journalist revealed numerous cases of fraud and corruption.	= deceit

Crime

vocabulary	dt. Bedeutung	English phrase	syn/opp
(to) harass harassment	belästigen Belästigung	The management issued a warning to male employees harassing women at work.	
incidence	Auftreten, Vorkommen	A rising incidence of sexual harassment was noted in the firm.	= occurrence
incident	Zwischenfall, Ereignis	"There has never been any incident of sexual harassment in our company", the manager said.	= case, event
juvenile delinquency	Jugend- kriminalität	crime committed by young people	= youth delinquency
lawbreaker	Gesetzes- brecher*in	a person who does not obey the law	= criminal
(to) mug	auf der Straße überfallen und ausrauben	to rob sb (esp. with violence) in a public place	= to hold up, to rob, to ambush
murder	Mord	The defendant was convicted of murder in three cases.	= homicide, manslaughter
murderer	Mörder*in	Jack the Ripper is the most mysterious murderer in British criminal history.	= killer
offence	Vergehen, Verbrechen	a crime; breaking the law	
offender	Täter*in, Straffällige*r	a person who committed a crime	= lawbreaker, delinquent
phishing	ein Passwort erschleichen	Criminals sent out faked emails phishing for people's username, password etc.	
pickpocket	Taschendieb*in	a person who steals from the pockets of others	

Crime

vocabulary	dt. Bedeutung	English phrase	syn/opp
precaution	Vorsicht(smaßnahme)	sth done in advance to avoid problems	
racketeer	Gauner*in, Gangster	a person who makes money through dishonest or illegal activities	
riot	Krawall	Riots broke out after the demonstration.	= disturbance, unrest
(to) rob	be-, ausrauben	The young criminal robbed the rich lady of her expensive jewellery.	
robber	Räuber*in	Kids used to play "cops and robbers".	
shoplifting	Ladendiebstahl	to steal sth from a shop while pretending to be a customer	
(to) stalk sb	jmd. nachstellen, sich anschleichen	to follow or approach (e.g. a celebrity, an enemy, an animal) without being seen	
(to) threaten threat	(be-)drohen Bedrohung	The gang threatened to beat him up if he didn't hand over his wallet.	
thug	Schlägertyp, Rowdy	a violent and often criminal person	
treason	Hochverrat	Mary, Queen of Scots, was executed for treason.	
troublemaker	Unruhestifter*in	a person who often causes difficulties or problems	
truancy (to) play truant	Schulschwänzen (die Schule) schwänzen	staying away from school without good reasons	= to skip school
victim	Opfer	The victim was interrogated by police.	
white-collar crime	Wirtschaftsverbrechen	stealing from a company or fiddling the books	

2 Drugs

vocabulary	dt. Bedeutung	English phrase	syn/opp
AA (Alcoholics Anonymous)	die Anonymen Alkoholiker	My uncle regularly goes to AA meetings because he wants to quit drinking.	
addict	Süchtige*r	Some drug addicts steal to finance their drugs.	
addiction	Sucht	Drug addiction has increased in our affluent society.	
alcoholic	Alkoholiker*in	An alcoholic is a person who is addicted to alcohol.	
alcoholism	Alkoholismus	Alcoholism is an underestimated problem.	
cocaine	Kokain	a powerful drug made from the coca plant	
(to) cure	heilen	Scientists are looking for ways to cure addiction.	
curiosity	Neugier	the strong desire to know or be informed about sth	≠ disinterest, indifference
(to) deny	leugnen	A big increase in drug-related crimes cannot be denied.	≠ to admit
	verweigern	Some drug addicts are denied adequate treatment.	≠ to permit, to grant
dependence	Abhängigkeit	a steady need	= addiction, craving
designer drug	synthetische Droge, Modedroge	At parties designer drugs like ecstasy or crystal meth were passed around.	
distribution	Verteilung, Vertrieb	supplying or giving out things to people	= supply, delivery

Crime **31**

Crime

vocabulary	dt. Bedeutung	English phrase	syn/opp
drug abuse	Drogenmissbrauch	Drug abuse among young people is on the rise.	
drug pusher	Drogenhändler*in	sb who sells drugs	= drug dealer
drug trafficking	Drogenhandel	dealing with drugs	
drug-related	mit Drogen in Zusammenhang stehend	Theft and robbery are often drug-related crimes.	
(to) eradicate eradication	ausrotten Ausrottung	to get rid of sth completely	= to eliminate, to wipe out
habit	Gewohnheit	I'm worried about my brother's drinking habits.	
harmful	schädlich	causing damage	= damaging, risky, unsafe
heroin	Heroin	a powerful drug made from poppies/opium	
(to) induce	verleiten, veranlassen	Peer pressure can induce young people to try drugs.	= to tempt
intoxicating	berauschend	making you feel drunk	= stimulating
lethal	tödlich	The young man died after a lethal injection.	= deadly, fatal, mortal
narcotics	Rauschgift	Heroin and cocaine are narcotics.	
narcotics agent	Rauschgiftfahnder*in	Narcotics agents received special training to stop new ways of smuggling drugs into the country.	
overdose	Überdosis	too much of a drug taken at one time	
(to) peddle drugs	mit Drogen handeln	He was jailed for peddling cocaine on the streets.	

vocabulary	dt. Bedeutung	English phrase	syn/opp
(to) sniff	*schnüffeln*	Kids of ten or even younger have begun sniffing glue.	= to breathe in, to inhale
supplier	*Lieferant*in*	person selling or making available sth that is needed by sb	
treatment	*Behandlung*	curing an illness or injury	
(to) withdraw **withdrawal**	*entziehen* *Entzug*	when sb stops doing or taking sth	
withdrawal symptoms	*Entzugserscheinungen*	the unpleasant feelings that an addict gets when he/she stops taking a drug/ alcohol/nicotine	
withdrawal treatment	*Entziehungskur, Entzug*	going on a cure to try to stop taking drugs/alcohol/ nicotine	

3 The court / Law

vocabulary	dt. Bedeutung	English phrase	syn/opp
accusation **(to) accuse**	*An-, Beschuldigung; Anklage* *beschuldigen*	a statement saying that sb has done sth morally wrong	
(to) acquit **acquittal**	*freisprechen* *Freispruch*	to declare sb to be not guilty of a crime	= to clear sb
allegation **(to) allege**	*Behauptung, Beschuldigung* *beschuldigen*	saying that sb has done sth illegal or wrong	
(to) appeal	*(bei Gericht) Berufung einlegen*	to apply to a superior court for a hearing of the whole or part of a case previously tried in a lower court	

vocabulary	dt. Bedeutung	English phrase	syn/opp
arbitrary	*willkürlich*	A democratic country needs a judiciary which is independent of the arbitrary power of a president or prime minister.	≠ lawful, rightful, legitimate
(to) arrest	*festnehmen, verhaften*	to take to the police station	≠ to release
attorney [US]	*Rechtsanwalt/ Rechtsanwältin*	a lawyer, esp. one qualified to act for clients in a law court	
bail	*Kaution, Bürgschaft*	The defendant was released on bail.	
ban (to) ban	*Verbot verbieten*	a formal prohibition	
barrister [UK]	*Gerichtsanwalt/ Gerichtsanwältin*	a lawyer representing the accused person in court	
capital punishment	*Todesstrafe*	Opponents of capital punishment are gaining more support in the USA.	= death penalty
caution	*Vorsicht*	Lawyers and judges should exercise caution.	
charge	*Beschuldigung, Anklage*	He was arrested on charges of burglary and theft.	
client	*Mandant*in, Klient*in*	a person who uses the services of a professional person or organisation, e. g. a lawyer	
(to) combat	*bekämpfen*	Severe sentences are expected to help combat crime.	= to fight, to battle, to struggle with
(to) condemn	*verdammen, verurteilen*	to express very strong disapproval	

Crime

vocabulary	dt. Bedeutung	English phrase	syn/opp
confession (to) confess	Geständnis gestehen	The murderer made a full confession to the police.	= admission of guilt ≠ denial
(to) confiscate	beschlagnahmen	In the 1950s Salinger's novel *The Catcher in the Rye* was confiscated in many schools.	
conviction (to) convict	Verurteilung überführen, verurteilen	Anyone found guilty of a crime has the right of appeal against conviction.	
court	Gerichtshof	a place where trials or other law cases are held; a law court	
courtroom	Gerichtssaal	a room in which the sittings of the court are held	
credibility	Glaubwürdigkeit	He has lied so often before, his credibility is damaged.	= reliability, integrity
cross-examination	Kreuzverhör (eines Zeugen/ einer Zeugin)	Under cross-examination the defendant admitted the crime.	
custody	Gewahrsam, Haft	The suspect will remain in custody until his trial.	= care, supervision
damages	Schadensersatz	The pharmaceutical firm had to pay $ 5 million in monetary damages.	
death penalty	Todesstrafe	The film *Dead man walking* is a protest against the death penalty.	= capital punishment
defence counsel [BE]	Verteidiger*in	lawyer who represents the defendant in a court case	= counsel for the defence
defendant	Angeklagte*r, Beschuldigte*r	The defendant admitted the crime.	

Crime

vocabulary	dt. Bedeutung	English phrase	syn/opp
(to) detain	in Haft behalten	to keep sb in an official place, e. g. a police station	= to keep in custody ≠ to release
error of justice	Justizirrtum	a wrong judgement or sentence	
evidence	Beweis(e)	He was arrested because the police had found enough evidence against him.	= proof
(to) execute	(ein Urteil) vollstrecken, hinrichten	to kill sb, esp. as a legal punishment	
execution	Hinrichtung	The execution took place at 5 a.m.	
federal legislation	Bundesgesetzgebung	laws imposed by the central government (i. e. in Washington)	
gaol [dʒeil]	Gefängnis	(old-fashioned for "jail") a place where criminals are kept as punishment	= prison, jail
human rights	Menschenrechte	Amnesty International fights for the respect of human rights.	
imprisonment	Haft-, Gefängnisstrafe	The accused was sentenced to five years imprisonment.	
indictment	Anklage	official accusation of an important person	
inmate	(Gefängnis-) Insasse/Insassin, Häftling	a person in prison	= prisoner
innocent	unschuldig	She claimed that she was absolutely innocent.	

Crime

vocabulary	dt. Bedeutung	English phrase	syn/opp
investigation	*(offizielle, polizeiliche) Untersuchung*	An official investigation of the incident has been ordered by the prime minister.	= enquiry
(to) investigate	*untersuchen*		
(to) jail	*einsperren*	to put a person behind bars	= to imprison ≠ to release from prison
juror	*der/die Geschworene*	a member of the jury	
jury	*die Geschworenen*	a group of people in a law court who decide whether the accused person is guilty or not guilty	
juvenile court	*Jugendgericht*	a court that deals with juvenile offenders and children beyond parental control or in need of care	
lawsuit	*Klage*	a case before a court	
lawyer	*Rechtsanwalt/ Rechtsanwältin*	a person trained and qualified in the law who does legal work for other people	
legal process	*Rechtsweg*	action through the processes of the law	
legislation	*Gesetzgebung*	a law or a series of laws	
liability	*Haftung, Haftpflicht*	legal responsibility for sth, especially costs or damages	
litigation	*Prozess, Rechtsstreit*	the process of prosecuting or defending a case in a civil court of law	
(to) monitor	*beobachten, kontrollieren*	CCTV cameras were installed to monitor public places.	
oath	*Eid*	a formal promise	

vocabulary	dt. Bedeutung	English phrase	syn/opp
penal penal law	Straf- Strafrecht	connected with or relating to punishment	
penalty	Strafe	The penalty for parking in the wrong place was increased to $ 50.	
perjury	Meineid	the crime of telling lies in court	
(to) plead	(vor Gericht) plädieren	The defendant pleaded "not guilty".	
probation probation officer	Bewährung Bewährungshelfer*in	keeping an official check on sb who has broken the law instead of sending him/her to prison	
prosecution (to) prosecute	strafrechtliche Verfolgung belangen, anklagen	Crime prevention is better than crime prosecution.	
prosecutor	Ankläger*in, Anklagevertreter*in	a person who conducts legal proceedings in a court of law, esp. on behalf of the public	
provision	Verordnung, Vorschrift	a legal statement or paragraph	
(to) read sb his/her rights	jdn. über seine Rechte belehren	The police must always read sb his/her rights before questioning.	
(to) release	freilassen	After three years he was released from prison.	
(to) sentence	verurteilen	to give or order a punishment	≠ to set free
severe	hart, streng, schwerwiegend	Will more severe sentences reduce the crime rate?	= strict, rigorous ≠ lenient, mild

Crime

vocabulary	dt. Bedeutung	English phrase	syn/opp
solicitor	*Rechtsanwalt/ Rechtsanwältin*	The young law student started practice in a firm of solicitors.	
state's attorney [US]	*Staatsanwalt, Staatsanwältin*	a public official who represents a state or the federal government in court	= district attorney [US], public prosecutor [UK]
(to) sue	*(auf Schadenersatz) verklagen*	to take legal action against sb in order to obtain compensation	
Supreme Court [US]	*Oberster Gerichtshof (in den USA)*	the highest court of law	
suspect	*(Tat-)Verdächtige*r*	a person who the police think has committed the crime	
suspicion	*Verdacht*	The policemen's suspicion was aroused when they saw the car drive away at full speed.	
(to) testify	*(vor Gericht) aussagen, bezeugen*	She refused to testify against her husband.	
trial	*Gerichtsverfahren, Prozess*	The defendant is entitled to a fair trial.	= court case
verdict	*Urteil*	The judge announced the verdict.	= judgement, sentence
witness	*Zeuge/Zeugin*	a person who appears in a court of law to say what he/she has seen or heard	

Politics

1 Constitution/Political system

vocabulary	dt. Bedeutung	English phrase	syn/opp
amendment	Änderung, Zusatz zur Verfassung	The Fifteenth Amendment (1870) to the US Constitution granted the right to vote to African Americans.	
(to) amend	berichtigen		
(to) appoint	ernennen	The president appoints ambassadors, ministers and consuls.	= to nominate
checks and balances	gegenseitige Kontrolle und gleichrangige Bedeutung	The US Constitution established checks and balances between the branches.	
(to) confirm	bestätigen	The Senate confirms the president's nominations.	
constitution	Verfassung	the law which determines the fundamental political principles of a government	= fundamental law
constitutional	verfassungsmäßig	In democratic countries the poor have a constitutional right to welfare.	
Constitutional Convention	verfassungsgebende Versammlung	The Constitutional Convention took place in Philadelphia in May 1787.	
constitutional monarchy	konstitutionelle Monarchie	In a constitutional monarchy the monarch is the head of state but his/her actions are controlled by the constitution.	
(to) consult	zurate ziehen	to get or ask advice from sb	

vocabulary	dt. Bedeutung	English phrase	syn/opp
declaration (to) declare	Erklärung verkünden	a formal announcement	
delegate	Delegierte*r, Abgesandte*r	a person appointed or elected to represent others	= representative, envoy
deliberately	absichtlich	The Constitution is deliberately silent on the question of education.	
(to) derive	von etw. stammen	The constitutional guarantee to religious freedom derives from the First Amendment.	= to stem from
(to) nominate nomination	ernennen Ernennung	The British monarch nominates the prime minister.	= to appoint
(to) perform	ausführen, erfüllen	A free press performs an important function in a democratic society.	
regulation	Vorschrift	There are no government regulations as to religious services at school.	= ruling, decree
separation of power	Gewaltenteilung	The separation of power is a principle of a democratic state.	
succession (to) succeed	Nachfolge, Erbfolge nachfolgen	a number of people or things that follow each other in time or order	
(to) vest power	Macht verleihen	The Constitution of 1787 vested executive power in a president.	

2 Executive/Government

vocabulary	dt. Bedeutung	English phrase	syn/opp
administration [US] (to) administer	Regierung; Verwaltung verwalten	the US president and his/her cabinet who govern the country	
agreement	Vereinbarung, Vertrag	The heads of state signed an agreement on economic aid.	
ambassador	Botschafter*in	a diplomat who represents his/her country in a foreign country	
armed forces	Streitkräfte	a country's army, air force and navy	
authority	Autorität, Vollmacht	the power or right to give orders or make decisions	
cabinet	Kabinett	The presidential cabinet comprises 14 members.	
capacity	Eigenschaft	The prime minister opened the meeting in her capacity as head of the government.	
ceremony	Feier, Zeremonie	a formal event	
challenger (to) challenge	Herausforderer/ Herausforderin herausfordern	Who will be the president's challenger in the next elections?	= rival, competitor
commander-in-chief	Oberbefehls-haber*in	The president of the United States is commander-in-chief of the armed forces.	
commission	Kommission, Ausschuss	a group of experts who have been chosen to solve a special problem	
(to) comprise	bestehen aus	How many counties does Ulster comprise?	= to consist of

Politics

vocabulary	dt. Bedeutung	English phrase	syn/opp
consent	Einwilligung, Zustimmung	Justices are appointed by the president with the consent of the Senate.	= approval ≠ refusal
coronation	Krönung	The coronation of Queen Elizabeth II in 1953 was the first major live TV broadcast in Britain.	
department	Abteilung, Ministerium	The presidential cabinet is made up of the heads of the federal departments.	
dictatorship	Diktatur	government by a dictator	
(to) dissolve dissolution	auflösen Auflösung	The king or queen dissolves parliament on the advice of the prime minister.	
embassy	Botschaft	official residence of an ambassador	
emperor, empress	Kaiser, Kaiserin	the ruler of an empire	
establishment	Bildung, Gründung, Errichtung	In 1921 the Irish civil war ended with the establishment of the Irish Free State.	
executive	ausführende Gewalt	The president is the head of the executive branch of the federal government.	= government
expenditure	Ausgabe, Aufwand	The government increased the defence expenditure.	
(to) exploit exploitation	ausbeuten, ausnutzen Ausbeutung	The native inhabitants were exploited by the white immigrants.	= to take advantage of, to use
extensive	ausgedehnt, umfassend	The government offers extensive information on current affairs.	= wide-ranging, far-reaching, detailed

vocabulary	dt. Bedeutung	English phrase	syn/opp
extract	*Auszug*	The document shows an extract from the country's Declaration of Independence.	= excerpt, passage
federal	*Bundes-*	The seat of the federal government of the USA is Washington.	
Foreign Office [BE]	*Außenministerium*	the government department which deals with connections with other countries	= State Department [US]
foreign policy/ foreign affairs	*Außenpolitik*	political matters that are connected with other countries	
foreign secretary	*Außenminister*in*	the head of the Foreign Office	= Secretary of State [US]
head of state	*Staatsoberhaupt*	The US president is head of state and head of the government at the same time.	
Home Office [BE]	*Innenministerium*	the government department which deals with matters inside the country	= Department of the Interior [US]
Home Secretary	*Innenminister*in*	the head of the Home Office	= Secretary of the Interior [US]
(to) impeach	*eines Amtes entheben*	The governor will be impeached for wrongful use of state money.	= to accuse, to put on trial, to prosecute
impeachment	*Amtsenthebung*		
inaugural address	*Amtsantrittsrede*	Education was the main subject in the president's inaugural address.	

vocabulary	dt. Bedeutung	English phrase	syn/opp
inauguration	Amtseinführung (bei US-Präsidenten)	Shortly after Abraham Lincoln's inauguration in 1860, the Civil War broke out.	
(to) inaugurate	(feierlich in ein Amt) einführen		
incompetent	unfähig	Incompetent politicians can cause lots of harm.	≠ competent
incumbent	amtierend	holding a particular post	
irrelevant	unerheblich, belanglos	beside the point	≠ relevant, important
(to) negotiate negotiation	verhandeln Verhandlung	The president has the power to negotiate treaties with other nations.	
oath of office	Amtseid	Lyndon Johnson took the oath of office on board the presidential jet, Air Force One.	
obsolete	veraltet	With the collapse of the Communist threat the original aims of the military alliance became obsolete.	= outmoded, out of date
(to) overthrow	stürzen, umstürzen	In 1961 the CIA supported plans to overthrow the Communist government in Cuba.	= to topple
(to) participate participation	teilnehmen Teilnahme	to take part in an activity	
politics	Politik	Well-educated people show a wider interest in politics.	
precaution	Vorsichtsmaßnahme	sth done in advance to avoid problems	= safety measure, safeguard
predecessor	Vorgänger*in	a person who had a job or position before sb else	≠ successor

Politics

vocabulary	dt. Bedeutung	English phrase	syn/opp
presidency	*Präsidentschaft*	the most powerful political position in the United States	
president-elect	*gewählter Präsident / gewählte Präsidentin (vor dem Amtsantritt)*	The president-elect has won the elections, but has not yet taken up office.	
presidential	*Präsidentschafts-, Präsidenten-*	Presidential elections take place every four years.	
prime minister	*Premierminister*in*	Margaret Thatcher (1979 – 1990) was Britain's first woman prime minister.	
(to) reign	*herrschen*	The British monarch reigns, but does not govern.	
(to) remove	*entfernen, beseitigen*	It is difficult to remove the president from office.	
removal	*Beseitigung*		
(to) reside	*wohnen*	The US president resides in the White House.	
residence	*Wohnsitz*		
(to) resign	*zurücktreten*	President Richard M. Nixon resigned in 1974.	
resignation	*Rücktritt*		
resolution	*Entschluss, Entschlossenheit*	formal statement of opinion	= declaration
(to) resolve	*etw. lösen, beschließen*		
royal	*königlich, Königs-*	Members of the British royal family are always in the news.	
sovereign	*Herrscher*in*	a king or queen	
staff	*Personal, Stab*	The president's visit to Dallas was arranged by his White House staff.	
summit	*Gipfel*	The president opened the World Summit on Sustainable Development.	

vocabulary	dt. Bedeutung	English phrase	syn/opp
(to) summon	einberufen	to call together	
term of office	Amtszeit, Amtsperiode	The president is elected by the voters for a fixed term of office.	
tyrant	Diktator*in	a person who has complete power in a country and uses it in a cruel and unfair way	= dictator
vice-president	Vizepräsident*in, stellvertretende*r Vorsitzende*r	Every four years Americans elect a president and a vice-president.	

3 Legislature / Parliament

vocabulary	dt. Bedeutung	English phrase	syn/opp
(to) adjourn	(eine Sitzung usw.) vertagen	to make a pause	= to postpone, to suspend
bill	Gesetzentwurf	US Congress approved a bill to increase federal spending.	
budget	Staatshaushalt, Etat	the financial plan of a country's income from taxes	
chamber	Kammer	The House of Lords is the upper chamber of the British legislature.	
committee	Ausschuss	A committee will work out suggestions to improve national health care.	
Congress [US]	Kongress	The US Congress consists of the Senate and the House of Representatives.	
(to) determine	bestimmen, festlegen	A date for the president's state visit to Germany has yet to be determined.	

Politics

vocabulary	dt. Bedeutung	English phrase	syn/opp
(to) empower	ermächtigen	to give (sb) the official or legal authority to do sth	= to authorise
(to) enact	(ein Gesetz) erlassen	The Belfast Agreement was enacted in November 1998.	
(to) entitle	berechtigen	Political refugees are entitled to temporary residence if they can prove that their lives are endangered.	
(to) exceed	überschreiten	to be greater than (a number or an amount)	
hereditary	erblich	For centuries Europe was largely ruled by hereditary monarchies.	
human rights	Menschenrechte	The UN and its family of organisations work to promote respect for human rights.	
issue	Streitfrage	an important topic of discussion	= problem
legislation	Gesetzgebung	Legislation passed in 1952 allows people of all races to become US citizens.	
legislative legislature	gesetzgebend Gesetzgebung	Congress makes up the legislative branch of government.	
(to) make a speech	eine Rede halten	The Home Secretary will make a speech on the benefits of immigration.	= to deliver a speech
Member of Parliament (MP)	Parlamentsabgeordnete*r	In Britain, a by-election is held when a Member of Parliament dies.	
minutes	Protokoll	a summary or record of what is said or decided in parliament	= transcription, record, notes

vocabulary	dt. Bedeutung	English phrase	syn/opp
motion	*parlamentarischer Antrag*	The opposition criticised the government's motion.	= proposal, proposition
(to) nationalise	*verstaatlichen*	to put an industry (steelworks, mines) or a company under the control of the government	≠ to denationalise, to privatise
(to) override	*sich hinwegsetzen über*	to use your authority to reject sb's decision	= to overrule
parliamentary	*parlamentarisch*	The Republic of Ireland is a parliamentary democracy.	
(to) pass a bill	*ein Gesetz verabschieden*	Congress passed a bill to reform the tax system.	= to adopt
policy	*Politik, Taktik*	The government's housing policy came under heavy attack.	= strategy, course of plan
politician	*Politiker*in*	Politicians try to persuade people to vote for them.	
previous	*vorherig, vorhergehend*	coming before; happening or existing before the event sb is talking about	= preceding ≠ subsequent
proposition	*Vorschlag, Antrag*	an idea or a plan of action	= proposal, plan, scheme
ratification	*Ratifizierung, Bestätigung*	The Equal Rights Amendment was passed by Congress and sent to the states for ratification.	= approval
(to) ratify	*ratifizieren, bestätigen*		
redundant	*überflüssig; arbeitslos*	not necessary because sb/sth else does the same thing	= superfluous, unnecessary
reputation	*Ruf*	Because of hooliganism Britain's reputation has suffered seriously both at home and abroad.	

vocabulary	dt. Bedeutung	English phrase	syn/opp
Senate	*Senat*	The US Senate is composed of 100 senators.	
session	*Sitzung, Sitzungsperiode*	In the UK, the monarch, as head of state, opens each new session of Parliament.	= meeting, conference, term
Speaker	*brit. Parlamentspräsident*in*	The Speaker of the House of Commons chairs meetings and controls discussions.	
(to) submit submission	*etw. vorlegen, unterbreiten Vorlage*	The new bill will be submitted to parliament for approval.	
(to) supervise supervision	*überwachen, beaufsichtigen Überwachung*	Parliament supervises finances and makes laws.	= to control, to oversee, to manage
taxation	*Besteuerung*	collecting money by taxes	
Tories	*brit. Konservative*	nickname of the Conservatives in Great Britain	
treaty	*Vertrag*	The Treaty of Maastricht establishing the European Union was signed in 1992.	
violation (to) violate	*Verletzung, Bruch verletzen*	Torture is a serious violation of human rights.	= breach, infringement
wing	*Flügel*	Sinn Fein is the political wing of the Provisional IRA.	

4 Judiciary/Law

vocabulary	dt. Bedeutung	English phrase	syn/opp
(to) balance	*Gleichgewicht herstellen*	The United States is a mix of cultures whose claims must be balanced against each other.	
consent	*Einwilligung, Zustimmung*	The president appoints judges with the consent of the Senate.	≠ refusal, veto, dissent
dissent	*Meinungsverschiedenheit*	For Jefferson, dissent was not only a right but also a necessity.	≠ consent
impartial	*unparteiisch*	not supporting one person or group more than another	= neutral, unbiased ≠ biased
judicial	*gerichtlich*	connected with a court of law, a judge or legal judgement	
judiciary	*Gerichtswesen, Richterstand*	The constitution guarantees the independence of the judiciary.	
justice	*Gerechtigkeit*	the fair treatment of people	≠ injustice
(to) nullify nullification	*für nichtig erklären* *Aufhebung*	The 14th amendment of the Constitution of the United States (1868) nullified a decision taken in 1857.	
(to) overturn	*kippen, widerrufen*	In 1954 the Supreme Court overturned the decision taken in 1896.	= to reverse ≠ to endorse
statutory	*gesetzlich*	The system of the presidential elections combines constitutional and statutory requirements.	

vocabulary	dt. Bedeutung	English phrase	syn/opp
Supreme Court [US]	*das Oberste Gericht*	the highest court in the US	
unanimous	*einstimmig*	The court came to a unanimous decision.	
unconstitutional	*verfassungswidrig*	The Supreme Court decided in 1954 that the "separate but equal" concept was unconstitutional.	
void	*null und nichtig*	An unconstitutional law is declared void.	= annulled

5 Elections

vocabulary	dt. Bedeutung	English phrase	syn/opp
ballot	*Wahl; Stimmzettel*	A secret ballot will be held next month.	= vote, election
by-election	*Nachwahl*	Because of the death of the MP for Erith a by-election was necessary.	
campaign	*Wahlkampf*	Most people who run for office limit their campaign to a year or two.	
(to) cast a vote	*abstimmen*	Can I cast my vote in writing or by telephone?	
constituency	*Wahlkreis*	In Britain, 650 MPs are elected, one in each constituency.	= electoral district
direct representation	*Mehrheitswahl*	Because of the British electoral system of direct representation, smaller parties have never played an important role.	
electoral system	*Wahlsystem*	The American electoral system is rather complex.	

vocabulary	dt. Bedeutung	English phrase	syn/opp
electorate	Wählerschaft	people who have the right to vote	= voters
eligible to	berechtigt	At 18 you are eligible to vote.	
FPTP (first-past-the-post)	Mehrheitswahl	another word for direct representation; an allusion to horse racing	
general election	allgemeine Wahl	In Britain, a general election takes place on a Thursday.	
landslide victory	überwältigender Wahlsieg	an election result which has brought an enormous shift from one party to another one	
local elections	Kommunalwahlen	The party of the prime minister lost many seats in the latest local elections.	
majority	Mehrheit	In order to win a constituency a candidate needs a simple majority of the votes.	≠ minority
majority vote	Mehrheitswahl	In Britain, MPs are elected by a majority vote.	
opponent	Gegner*in	The Republican candidate will face his Democratic opponent in three television debates.	= rival, challenger, adversary
overwhelming	überwältigend	The new bill will receive overwhelming support from all parties.	
platform	Parteiprogramm	a compilation of the aims of a political party	
poll	Umfrage, Wahl	According to the latest poll, Labour will lose many seats in the coming election.	

Politics

vocabulary	dt. Bedeutung	English phrase	syn/opp
polling booth	*Wahlkabine*	a small, partly enclosed place in a polling station where people vote secretly	
polling day	*Wahltag*	Polling day in Britain is always a Thursday.	
polling station	*Wahllokal*	a building where people go to vote in an election	
precinct [US]	*Wahlkreis, Wahlbezirk*	a small electoral district of a city or town	
presidential election	*Präsidentschaftswahl*	Waiting for the results of the presidential election in 2000 lasted longer than ever before.	
primaries	*Vorwahlen*	In primaries, party members choose their presidential candidate.	
proportional representation	*Verhältniswahl*	The system of proportional representation gives smaller parties a fairer chance to be represented in parliament.	
representative	*Vertreter*in*	a person who has been chosen to speak or vote for the interests of a group	
(to) run for president	*(für die Präsidentschaft) kandidieren*	Very early in his life, John F. Kennedy decided that one day he would run for president.	
splinter party	*Splitterpartei*	A splinter party has broken away from a major political party.	
turnout	*Wahlbeteiligung*	the number of people who actually vote in an election	
vote	*Abstimmung*	There will be a vote on the government's bill next week.	

From Empire to the EU and Brexit

1 Empire

vocabulary	dt. Bedeutung	English phrase	syn/opp
acquisition (to) acquire	Erwerb erwerben	The First British Empire began with the acquisition of territories overseas.	
administration	Verwaltung	The colonies were under the administration of the British.	
affairs	Angelegenheiten, Sachen	commercial, professional, public, or personal matters	
arrogant	hochmütig, arrogant	Very often the British "masters" behaved in an arrogant way.	= disdainful, haughty, overbearing
benefit	Vorteil, Nutzen	Do you think the British rule was also a benefit to the colonised countries?	
(to) colonise	kolonisieren	to send a group of settlers to a place and establish political control over it	
(to) conduct	durchführen, leiten, betreiben	British firms conducted their business in the new colonies.	
(to) despise	verachten, verschmähen	The native population was often despised by the white colonialists – and vice versa.	= to look down, to scorn ≠ to appreciate, to esteem
disparity	Ungleichheit, Unvereinbarkeit	Imperialism led to a disparity of wealth between Britain and its colonies.	= disproportion, inequality

vocabulary	dt. Bedeutung	English phrase	syn/opp
diversity	Vielfalt	Despite the diversity of its members, the Commonwealth can act globally.	≠ uniformity; identity
Empire	das britische Weltreich	The First British Empire began to develop in the 16th century.	
(to) establish	gründen, bilden, einrichten	The British established a new law system in the colonies.	≠ to abolish
(to) exert	(eine Kraft, einen Einfluss) ausüben	The new rulers exerted a powerful influence.	= to exercise
exploitation	Ausbeutung, Ausnutzung	The colonists' primary aim was the exploitation of natural resources.	
(to) exploit	ausbeuten, ausnutzen		
(to) extend	verlängern, ausdehnen	to make or become longer	
extension	Ausdehnung, Verlängerung		
heritage	Erbe	A large part of immigration to Britain had to do with its imperial heritage.	= inheritance
imperial	kaiserlich; Empire-, des Empires	George Orwell served in the Imperial Police in British-ruled Burma.	
(to) impose	(eine Steuer usw.) auferlegen; (eine Geldstrafe) verhängen	The British parliament imposed a new tax on paper.	
imposition	Einführung; Verhängung		
indigenous	einheimisch	The indigenous population was regarded as second-class.	= native

From Empire to the EU and Brexit

vocabulary	dt. Bedeutung	English phrase	syn/opp
manufactured goods	*Industriewaren*	The British used the Empire as a market for their manufactured goods.	
merchant	*Kaufmann/ Kauffrau*	a buyer and seller of commodities	= trader, businessman/ -woman
mill	*Fabrik, Textilfabrik*	As a young man David Livingstone worked in a cotton mill in Glasgow.	= factory, works
monopoly	*Monopol*	A protest against the trade monopoly of the East India Company resulted in the Boston Tea Party in 1773.	= trust, syndicate
native	*einheimisch*	The native population was subdued by the colonists.	= indigenous ≠ alien, foreign
(to) neglect	*vernachlässigen*	to give little or no attention	≠ to cherish, to cultivate
outcome	*Ergebnis*	Britain's loss of the North American colonies was the outcome of experience learnt the hard way in 1776.	= result, consequence
persecution (to) persecute	*Verfolgung verfolgen*	The Pilgrim Fathers were searching for a place to express their faith freely without persecution.	
quest	*Suche*	The quest for new colonies was intensified in the 17th century.	= search
raw materials	*Rohstoffe*	Raw materials from the colonies, such as sugar and cotton, were manufactured in the factories in England.	
(to) reign	*regieren, herrschen*	to possess or exercise sovereign power	

vocabulary	dt. Bedeutung	English phrase	syn/opp
(to) rule	regieren	The British ruled over great parts of the world.	= to govern
ruthless	unbarmherzig, gnadenlos	The revolt was suppressed with ruthless force.	= merciless
separation (to) separate	Trennung trennen	The First Empire came to an end with the separation of the American colonies from the British crown in 1783.	
status	Rechtsstellung, Status	The British rejected India's demands for dominion status.	
superiority	Überlegenheit	The colonists believed in the superiority of the "white race".	≠ inferiority
supremacy	Vormachtstellung	the position of being first in influence or power	
trading company	Handelsgesellschaft	The trading companies enjoyed many privileges.	
(to) transcend	über etw. hinausgehen	to rise above or go beyond the limits	= to surpass, to exceed
unchecked	unkontrolliert	Britain's unchecked quest for power is responsible for the exploitation of the colonies.	
undisputed	unumstritten	In the 19th century Britain's position in the world was undisputed.	
(to) yield sth to sb	etw. an jdn. abgeben	The British failed to yield power to the American colonists.	

2 Commonwealth

vocabulary	dt. Bedeutung	English phrase	syn/opp
(to) acknowledge	anerkennen	to recognise the rights, authority, or status of sb or sth	≠ to ignore, to deny
alliance	Bündnis	connection between families, states, parties etc.	= coalition
Commonwealth	das (britische) Commonwealth	political organisation consisting of nations loyal to the British monarch	
dominion	Herrschaftsgebiet, brit. Dominion (selbstständiges Land des Commonwealth)	The British gave Canada dominion status in 1867.	
(to) emerge	entstehen, hervorgehen	The multiracial Commonwealth began to emerge after the First World War.	≠ to disappear
independence movement	Unabhängigkeitsbewegung	Gandhi became the key figure in the independence movement in India.	
independent	unabhängig	free from control by others	= free, autonomous, sovereign
interior	intern, innere, Innen-	Britain's former colonies were granted home rule to decide about their interior affairs themselves.	≠ exterior
loose	lose	The Commonwealth is a loose association of about 50 states.	
membership	Mitgliedschaft	In 1949, India decided to continue its membership in the Commonwealth.	

vocabulary	dt. Bedeutung	English phrase	syn/opp
privilege	*Vorrecht, Privileg*	a right granted as a particular advantage or favour	
selfish	*selbstsüchtig*	The Commonwealth is not a selfish organisation.	= egoistic, self-interested
sovereign	*souverän, eigenständig*	The Commonwealth includes more than fifty sovereign nations and several dependencies.	= autonomous, independent
(to) transform	*etw./jdn. verwandeln*	The British transformed their Empire into the Commonwealth of Nations.	= to change, to convert
voluntary	*freiwillig*	The Commonwealth is a voluntary association of independent states.	≠ involuntary, obligatory

3 European Union and Brexit

vocabulary	dt. Bedeutung	English phrase	syn/opp
(to) abolish **abolition**	*abschaffen, aufheben* *Abschaffung*	to put an end to sth	= to remove, to do away with
(to) achieve **achievement**	*erlangen, erreichen* *Leistung, Errungenschaft, Erfolg*	It seems extremely difficult to achieve an agreement on a common agricultural policy.	= to attain
(to) admit **admittance / admission**	*zulassen, etw. zugeben* *Einlass, Eintritt, Zutritt*	The UK, Denmark and Ireland were admitted to the European Economic Community in 1973.	≠ to exclude
(to) adopt	*annehmen*	Other EU countries might adopt the euro in the future.	
agriculture	*Landwirtschaft*	Agriculture is a very difficult field in EU politics.	

From Empire to the EU and Brexit

vocabulary	dt. Bedeutung	English phrase	syn/opp
(to) apply for application	sich bewerben um Bewerbung	Britain first applied for membership in the EEC in 1961 – but was not admitted.	
bailout	Rettungsaktion	To cope with the financial crisis, several European banks had to ask the governments for a bailout.	= (financial) rescue
Brexit	Brexit	combination of the words "Britain" and "exit" – refers to Britain's decision to leave the European Union	
Brexiteer	Brexit-Befürworter*in	person in favour of Brexit, i. e. of Britain leaving the EU	
(to) cease	aufhören	By 1980, the EEC had ceased to develop further.	= to stop, to discontinue
civil servant	Beamte*r	A civil servant is a person who works for the government.	
(to) commit commitment	sich verpflichten Verpflichtung	In the treaties the member states also committed themselves to improve the effectiveness of a Common Foreign and Security Policy (CFSP).	
community	Gemeinschaft	The new members added significantly to the size of the community.	
competition (to) compete	Wettbewerb, Konkurrenz konkurrieren	Many managers thought that more competition would cause higher unemployment.	
confederation	Bündnis	an organisation which consists of a number of parties or groups	= alliance

vocabulary	dt. Bedeutung	English phrase	syn/opp
Council of Ministers	Ministerrat	The French finance minister Jacques Delors submitted to the Council of Ministers the idea to create a single market.	
counterweight	Gegengewicht	The EU was created as a counterweight to the large consumer markets in Japan and the USA.	= counterbalance
dilemma	Zwangslage	a situation in which a difficult choice has to be made between two or more bad alternatives	= predicament
EC (European Community)	EG (Europäische Gemeinschaft)	name of the European Union between 1973 and 1993	
economic policy	Wirtschaftspolitik	The total number of new jobs might be higher if the government pursued a different economic policy.	
EEC (European Economic Community)	EWG (Europäische Wirtschaftsgemeinschaft)	name of the original alliance of six European countries begun in 1957	
efficiency	Leistungsfähigkeit	The governments must improve the efficiency of the EU.	= effectiveness, performance
emergency measure	Notmaßnahme	The EU took emergency measures to protect the value of the euro.	
enlargement	Vergrößerung	The representatives of the EU discussed the enlargement of the union.	= extension
EU (European Union)	EU (Europäische Union)	The Treaty of Maastricht (1993) marks the beginning of the EU.	

From Empire to the EU and Brexit

vocabulary	dt. Bedeutung	English phrase	syn/opp
Eurosceptic	*euroskeptisch, Euroskeptiker*in*	Eurosceptic parties like the right-wing UK Independence Party campaigned in favour of Brexit.	
(to) evolve	*(sich weiter-) entwickeln*	to develop gradually	
evolution	*Entwicklung, Evolution*		
improvement	*Verbesserung, Fortschritt*	Many EU citizens welcomed the improvements in the free movement of people.	
influential	*einflussreich*	The plan of extending the EU was strongly supported by influential managers.	
(to) intend	*beabsichtigen*	The member countries intended to agree on a common defence policy.	= to plan
isolation	*Isolation, Absonderung, Trennung*	without relation to other people or things	
(to) isolate	*trennen*		
merger	*Fusion, Zusammenlegung*	A merger of two companies often results in a loss of jobs.	= amalgamation, union
monetary	*Währungs-*	In 2002, the euro became the monetary unit of 12 European countries.	
(to) predict	*voraussagen*	Opinion polls on Britain's EU referendum in 2016 predicted a close race between "Remain" and "Leave".	= to forecast
prediction	*Voraussage, Vorhersage*		
presidency	*Präsidentschaft*	Each EU member state takes over the presidency for six months.	

vocabulary	dt. Bedeutung	English phrase	syn/opp
prospect	*Aussicht*	Business managers welcomed the prospect of increased trade.	= outlook, perspective
(to) pursue **pursuit / pursuance**	*verfolgen, betreiben* *Verfolgung*	The government pursues a strict financial policy.	= to follow
quota	*(Einfuhr-) Kontingent*	The EEC countries did away with all quotas between the member countries.	
referendum	*Volksentscheid*	In a referendum in 2016, 51.9 % of British people voted in favour of leaving the EU.	
(to) sign	*unterzeichnen*	The Treaty of Rome was signed in March 1957.	
single currency	*Binnenwährung*	The single currency has made it easier to compare prices in Europe.	
single market	*Binnenmarkt*	Jacques Delors developed the plan for the creation of a single market.	
stimulus	*Reiz, Ansporn*	The preparation of the single currency provided the stimulus to cut inflation.	= incentive
(to) submit	*unterbreiten, vorlegen*	The Council of Ministers will submit a new proposal to increase the number of members.	
survey	*Untersuchung, Umfrage*	Surveys showed that the topics of immigration and national sovereignty influenced the outcome of the Brexit referendum.	= study, poll

vocabulary	dt. Bedeutung	English phrase	syn/opp
target	*Ziel*	In the Treaty of Rome of 1957, the founding countries set themselves a clear target.	= aim, objective
tariffs [Pl.]	*Zolltarife, Zölle*	The EEC countries reduced tariffs between member countries.	
trade agreement	*Handelsabkommen*	Representatives of the EU and Britain met to talk about trade agreements after Brexit.	= trade deal
treaty	*(Staats-)Vertrag*	Six countries (France, Italy, Belgium, Germany, Luxembourg and the Netherlands) signed the Treaty of Rome in 1957.	= agreement, convention
turning point	*Wende, Wendepunkt*	The Treaty of Maastricht (1993) was a turning point in the development of the EU.	

World affairs

1 War and peace

vocabulary	dt. Bedeutung	English phrase	syn/opp
(to) advance	vorrücken, vordringen	The general's army managed to advance even further.	= to move forward ≠ to recede
(to) advocate	verteidigen, befürworten	The Prime Minister seems to advocate a reduction of defence costs.	= to support, to back
(to) affect	beeinträchtigen, sich auswirken auf	The relationship between the two countries was affected by the discussion on human rights.	
alliance	Bündnis	An alliance is a relationship in which two or more people or groups work together for some purpose.	= coalition
ally	Verbündete*r, Alliierte*r	The USA and its European allies met for discussions in Brussels.	
armament	Aufrüstung, Rüstung	We talk of armament when a country increases the number of its weapons.	
armistice	Waffenstillstand	An armistice is an agreement between two countries at war with one another to stop fighting.	= truce
armour	Rüstung	An armour is a defensive covering for the body, often made of metal.	
arms	Waffen	One can hardly think of more destructive weapons than nuclear arms.	= weapons

vocabulary	dt. Bedeutung	English phrase	syn/opp
arms control	*Rüstungskontrolle*	The two superpowers agreed to introduce mutual arms control.	
arms race	*Wettrüsten, Rüstungswettlauf*	Because of the arms race a lot of money is wasted.	
(to) assign	*bestimmen, (Aufgabe) zuweisen*	The government assigned the army to control the streets at night.	
balance of power	*Machtgleichgewicht*	During the Cold War people thought that only a balance of power could guarantee peace in Europe.	
(to) betray	*verraten*	to reveal to an enemy important information	
bloodshed	*Blutvergießen*	There was no evidence of bloodshed or attack.	
casualties	*Verluste, Opfer*	No casualties were reported.	= victims, losses
ceasefire	*Feuerpause, Waffenruhe*	an agreement to stop fighting	
ceaseless	*endlos*	without stopping	= unending, continuous
(to) compensate for	*entschädigen für*	The army has to compensate farmers for damage done to their land during manoeuvres.	= to repay
conscientious objector	*Wehrdienstverweigerer/ Wehrdienstverweigerin*	In Austria, conscientious objectors have to do community service instead of military service.	
conscript	*Wehrpflichtige*r*	A conscript usually serves the army more unwillingly than a volunteer or professional.	

World affairs

vocabulary	dt. Bedeutung	English phrase	syn/opp
cowardice	Feigheit	He despised them for their cowardice and ignorance.	≠ courage
(to) cut costs	Kosten senken/reduzieren	It is the government's intention to cut defence costs.	= to reduce, to trim
(to) declare war	Krieg erklären	The Japanese declared war on the USA after the attack on Pearl Harbor in December 1941.	
defence expenditure	Verteidigungsausgaben	Many governments have increased their defence expenditure.	
(to) defy	sich auflehnen, widersetzen	The officer defied the order of the commanding general.	= to resist
(to) deploy deployment	(Truppen) einsetzen Aufmarsch	The government deployed troops to avoid a civil war.	
detente	Entspannung	In the 1970s and 80s, detente created a live and let live attitude in Europe.	
(to) deteriorate deterioration	sich verschlechtern Verschlechterung	Relations between the opposing groups have deteriorated sharply.	= to become worse
deterrent	Abschreckung	Some people think nuclear weapons are a deterrent against war.	
disarmament	Abrüstung	a process in which countries agree to reduce the number of weapons they have	
dissolution (to) dissolve	Auflösung auflösen	The defeated army fled in dissolution.	
durable	dauerhaft	Can a durable peace be achieved?	= lasting, permanent, stable ≠ fragile, weak

World affairs

vocabulary	dt. Bedeutung	English phrase	syn/opp
gloomy / gloom	trostlos, Hoffnungslosigkeit	Pessimists expect a gloomy future as far as social peace is concerned.	= dark, sad, pessimistic
incessant	ununterbrochen	sth going on without interruption	= ceaseless, constant
insoluble	unlösbar	sth that cannot be solved or explained	
(to) instruct	anweisen	The officer instructed his men which route to take.	= to direct, to order
invincible	unbesiegbar	too powerful to be conquered or defeated	
(to) maintain	aufrechterhalten	Troops were sent in to maintain public order.	= to keep up, to preserve
martial law	Kriegs-, Standrecht	The country has now spent more than eight years under martial law.	
mercenary	Söldner*in	a soldier hired into foreign service	
national service	Wehrdienst	Compulsory national service was abolished in Germany in 2011.	= military service, conscription
nuclear disarmament	atomare Abrüstung	Nuclear disarmament on a world-wide scale was of vital importance in the 1980s.	≠ atomic war
nuclear war	Atomkrieg	If a nuclear war broke out, it would mean the end of the world as we know it.	= atomic war
nuclear weapons	Atomwaffen	All nuclear weapons should be banned and destroyed.	= atomic arms
obedience / (to) obey	Gehorsam, gehorchen, folgen	Obedience is necessary for an army to function.	

World affairs

vocabulary	dt. Bedeutung	English phrase	syn/opp
(to) outnumber	*an Zahl überlegen sein, übertreffen*	In this group the men outnumber the women by four to one.	
policy of detente	*Entspannungspolitik*	The president's policy of detente led to an agreement with the USSR.	
(to) preserve	*erhalten, bewahren*	UN troops (Blue Helmets) were sent to the area to prevent aggression and preserve the peace.	= to conserve, to maintain, to keep up
(to) prevail	*die Oberhand gewinnen*	"We will prevail in the war", the president exclaimed.	= to succeed, to triumph ≠ to fail
process	*Prozess, Verfahren, Vorgang*	The peace process has come to a standstill.	
professional armed forces	*Berufsstreitkräfte*	Britain has had professional armed forces since 1960.	
raid	*(überraschender) Angriff*	Thousands were killed in the air-raid.	
(to) ravage	*verwüsten, Schaden anrichten*	Public buildings were ravaged by looters and plunderers.	= to devastate
reinforcement	*Verstärkung*	As a matter of reinforcement the government sent more troops to the war zone.	
(to) retreat	*sich zurückziehen*	After losing the first battle, the army had to retreat.	= to withdraw
shelter	*Schutz(-raum)*	During the Second World War thousands of Londoners sought shelter in underground stations.	
shortage	*Knappheit*	Wars have always been accompanied by a shortage of food and water.	≠ surplus

vocabulary	dt. Bedeutung	English phrase	syn/opp
(to) smash	zerschmettern, zerschlagen	During the revolt people were injured, cars burned and property was smashed.	= to break, to shatter, to destroy
(to) spill blood	Blut vergießen	The blood of innocent people was spilled.	
(to) summon	zusammenrufen, einberufen	to demand or request the presence or service of sb	
supply	Nachschub	The armed forces waited for the supply sent out on ferryboats.	
(to) suppress suppression	unterdrücken Unterdrückung	Troops were called out to suppress the rebellion.	= to oppress
surrender	Kapitulation, Übergabe, Aufgabe	The army tried to starve their enemies into surrender.	= capitulation
traitor	Verräter*in	sb who is not loyal to his/her country or to a group to which he/she belongs	
unconditional	bedingungslos	In 1945, the allies demanded the unconditional surrender of the German army.	
unrelenting	unerbittlich	Members of the rifle association try to explain their unrelenting opposition to gun control.	
valour	Heldenmut	strength of mind or spirit that enables a person to cope with a dangerous situation	≠ cowardliness, fear
(to) vanquish	besiegen, überwinden	They managed to vanquish all their enemies.	= to conquer, to defeat
volunteer	Freiwillige*r	"One volunteer is better than ten conscripts."	

World affairs 75

vocabulary	dt. Bedeutung	English phrase	syn/opp
warfare	*Kriegsführung*	Atomic warfare must be avoided at all costs.	
warrior	*Krieger*in*	This book is about the noble king, his bravest warrior and the greatest battles.	= fighter, combatant
(to) withdraw	*(sich) zurückziehen*	The British had to withdraw their troops from all the countries east of Suez.	= to retreat
wound [u:]	*Wunde*	an injury to the body from violence or an accident	

2 The world after 9/11

vocabulary	dt. Bedeutung	English phrase	syn/opp
aftermath	*Folge, Nachwirkungen*	In the aftermath of the terrorist attack, security measures were intensified.	
airstrike	*Luftangriff*	Jets carried out airstrikes on chemical facilities.	= air attack, air raid
animosity	*Abneigung*	a deep-rooted feeling of dislike	= hostility, enmity ≠ liking
assault	*Angriff, Anschlag*	The assault was carried out by seven gunmen.	= attack
(to) assert	*bestätigen, versichern*	Officials asserted that a chemical attack killed at least 70 people.	= to affirm, to declare
atrocity	*Gräueltat*	(an act of) great evil, esp. cruelty	
(to) attribute to	*zuschreiben, zurückführen auf*	The terror attack was attributed to Al-Qaeda.	

vocabulary	dt. Bedeutung	English phrase	syn/opp
bigot	*Fanatiker*in*	sb with unreasonable ideas about politics, religion or race who will not accept the opinions of anyone who disagrees	= fanatic, maniac
(to) boast	*prahlen*	to exaggerate one's abilities	= to brag
candlelight vigil	*Mahnwache*	A candlelight vigil was held to commemorate the victims of the attack.	
civil liberties	*Freiheitsrechte, bürgerliche Freiheiten*	We must monitor terrorist activities and, at the same time, respect civil liberties.	
(to) claim lives	*das Leben kosten, Menschenleben fordern*	The terrorist attack claimed the lives of innocent people.	
(to) combat	*bekämpfen*	To combat terrorism, the authorities curtailed civil liberties.	
(to) condemn	*verurteilen, verdammen*	to say that sth is completely unacceptable	
(to) condone	*(stillschweigend) dulden*	to tolerate or allow sth which is morally wrong to continue	
(to) confine	*beschränken*	Terrorist acts were not confined to members of what was called the Islamic State.	= to restrict
cover name	*Deckname*	a name concealing the true identity of a person	
credibility	*Glaubwürdigkeit*	combination of respect and trust	

vocabulary	dt. Bedeutung	English phrase	syn/opp
crusade	*Kreuzzug*	George W. Bush's "crusade" against terrorism began with the invasion of Iraq in March 2003.	
cyberterrorism	*Cyberterrorismus*	Cyberterrorism is an immediate threat to our safety.	
(to) deny	*abstreiten*	to state that sth is not true	≠ to acknowledge, to admit
Department of Homeland Security (DHS) [US]	*Heimatschutzministerium (USA)*	The Department of Homeland Security was established in response to the 9/11 attacks.	
(to) designate	*bereitstellen*	More funds have been designated for counter-terrorism efforts.	
(to) detain	*festhalten*	Terrorist suspects were detained at the US Naval Station Guantanamo Bay.	
drone	*Drohne (unbemanntes Luftfahrzeug)*	Border control agents use drones to hunt down terrorists and illegal aliens.	
(to) emerge	*auftauchen, entstehen, aufkommen*	More recently, "lone wolf" terrorists have emerged as the new face of terrorism.	≠ to disappear
(to) erupt	*ausbrechen*	Huge fireballs erupted when the jets crashed into the Twin Towers.	= to break out
(to) exceed	*übersteigen, überschreiten*	The cruelty of the attack exceeds the imagination.	= surpass
(to) hijack	*kapern, entführen*	Two hijacked aircrafts crashed into the World Trade Center.	
human rights	*Menschenrechte*	Harsh interrogation measures violated human rights.	

vocabulary	dt. Bedeutung	English phrase	syn/opp
(to) incite	*aufstacheln, anstiften*	The leader's hate speech incited the crowd to violence against ethnic minorities.	
incitement	*Anstiftung, Aufwiegelung*		
inevitable	*unvermeidlich*	Some political leaders see the outbreak of more violence in the Middle East as inevitable.	≠ avoidable
(to) inflict	*jdm. etw. zufügen*	The air attacks inflicted a lot of suffering on the civilian population.	
(to) infringe on	*verstoßen gegen, verletzen*	Additional security steps have infringed on the right to privacy.	
(to) infuriate	*jdn. wütend machen*	to make sb very angry	
(to) intimidate	*einschüchtern*	to put fear into sb	= to frighten
issue	*Streitfrage, Problem*	a problem or political decision	
menace	*Bedrohung*	The terrorist menace has spread worldwide.	= threat, peril
(to) monitor	*überwachen, kontrollieren*	The National Security Agency (NSA) monitored communication on the Internet illegally.	
perfidious	*heimtückisch, gemein*	The prisoners were subjected to perfidious forms of torture.	
pre-emptive strike	*Präventivschlag*	The president's military advisers supported the strategy of pre-emptive strikes.	
prejudice	*Vorurteil*	having an unreasonable or unfair idea about sb or sth	= bias

World affairs

vocabulary	dt. Bedeutung	English phrase	syn/opp
refugee shelter	Flüchtlingslager, Aufnahmelager	Last month fewer people were registered at the refugee shelter.	= refugee camp
remedy	Heilmittel, Lösung	a way of curing sth	= cure
repentance	Reue	the state of being sorry for the wrong one has done	= remorse
rogue state	Schurkenstaat	The president called countries which supported terrorists "rogue states".	
screening	Untersuchung, Sicherheitsüberprüfung	High-tech screening of passengers and baggage at airports has led to delays.	
scrutiny	(genaue) Überprüfung	Scrutiny of travellers from Middle Eastern countries has been intensified.	
stronghold	Hochburg, Stützpunkt	French troops captured a rebel stronghold in Mali.	
suicide attack	Selbstmordattentat	The Secret Service made suggestions about how to combat suicide attacks.	= suicide bombing
suicide terrorist	Selbstmordattentäter*in	Concerns have increased that nuclear power plants might become possible targets for suicide terrorists.	
surveillance	Überwachung, Überwachungs-	The border between Mexico and the USA is monitored by surveillance cameras.	
(to) target	abzielen auf, ins Visier nehmen	Islamist militant movements targeted the French embassy.	
vengeance	Vergeltung, Rache	After the September 11 attacks, the president promised vengeance.	

vocabulary	dt. Bedeutung	English phrase	syn/opp
warrant	*Durchsuchungsbefehl, Haftbefehl*	Police were allowed to search apartments and houses without warrants.	

3 Ireland – The Troubles

vocabulary	dt. Bedeutung	English phrase	syn/opp
boundary	*Grenze*	a line which marks the limits of an area	
civil war	*Bürgerkrieg*	The Irish civil war led to the partition of the island in 1920.	
commemoration	*Gedenken*	Protestant Unionists march through Catholic areas in commemoration of the Battle of the Boyne in 1690.	
compromise	*Kompromiss*	settlement of differences by mutual concessions	
(to) conclude	*(eine Vereinbarung) schließen*	The Good Friday Agreement was concluded on April 10, 1998.	
(to) decommission	*abgeben, ausmustern*	to hand over arms to the authorities	
direct rule	*Verwaltung Nordirlands durch die britische Regierung*	Direct rule by the British began in 1972.	
dominant	*vorherrschend, tonangebend*	Protestants in Ulster have always held a dominant position.	= superior, leading
DUP (Democratic Unionist Party)	*radikal protestantische/probritische Partei in Nordirland*	party which represents unionist interests	

World affairs **81**

vocabulary	dt. Bedeutung	English phrase	syn/opp
Eire	*Irland*	the Gaelic name for Ireland, the official name of the Republic of Ireland from 1937 to 1949	
fragile	*zerbrechlich, brüchig, unsicher*	Any agreement in Ulster is rather fragile.	= delicate, frail ≠ tough
Good Friday Agreement	*Karfreitagsabkommen*	On Good Friday 1998, all parties involved signed an agreement that peace can only be achieved without violence.	
grievance	*Beschwerde, Klage*	a cause for complaint	
home rule	*Selbstverwaltung*	The campaign for Irish home rule began in the late 19th century.	
Home Rule Act	*Gesetz zur politischen Selbstverwaltung Nordirlands*	The Home Rule Act was passed in 1914.	
incompatible	*unvereinbar*	Political observers think that the views of the Protestants and the Catholics are incompatible.	= conflicting, discrepant ≠ compatible
IRA (Irish Republican Army)	*IRA (Irisch-Republikanische Armee)*	terrorist organisation whose aim is to achieve reunification of Northern Ireland and the Republic	
irreconcilable	*unvereinbar, unversöhnlich*	The political views of the Protestants and the Catholics in Ulster are irreconcilable.	= incompatible
loyalist	*Befürworter der politischen Union zwischen GB und Nordirland*	in Ulster: the Protestants; they are seen as loyal to Britain	

vocabulary	dt. Bedeutung	English phrase	syn/opp
mutual	*gegenseitig, beiderseitig*	The Good Friday Agreement has not turned mutual dislike into cooperation.	
(to) negotiate	*verhandeln*	to try to reach an agreement by talking with the other party	
(to) partition	*(ein Land) teilen*	to divide into two or more parts	
Plantation	*Kolonisierung, Besiedlung*	Plantation of Ulster: settlement of Scots and Englishmen	
predominance	*Vorherrschaft, Überlegenheit*	Ulster has long been an area of Protestant predominance.	
Provos (Provisionals)	*Angehörige der IRA*	members of the Provisional Irish Republican Army (IRA)	
reconciliation (to) reconcile	*Versöhnung, Aussöhnung versöhnen*	There are still hopes for reconciliation between Roman Catholics and Protestants.	
(to) retain	*behalten*	Protestant loyalists are determined to retain the constitutional link with London.	= to keep, to continue
reunification (to) reunify	*Wiedervereinigung wiedervereinigen*	The reunification of the whole island is an important element of the Irish constitution.	
sectarian	*konfessionell bedingt, sektiererisch*	Provos are responsible for a large number of sectarian killings.	

vocabulary	dt. Bedeutung	English phrase	syn/opp
sectarianism	Sektierertum	strong, even violent support of a particular religious denomination and its political representation	
settlement	Einigung	Further efforts were made to achieve a political settlement.	= agreement
Sinn Fein	Sinn Fein (Irish Gaelic: "we ourselves")	the political party representing Catholics in Northern Ireland	
Ulster	Nordirland	Ulster is the northern province of Ireland; six of its nine counties belong to the United Kingdom.	
Ulster Unionists	nordirische Unionisten	Protestants who are in favour of the union of Northern Ireland and Great Britain	
UUP (Ulster Unionist Party)	Protestantenpartei Nordirlands (probritische Partei)	party in Northern Ireland which represents unionist interests	

Economy

1 Economic policy and business economics

vocabulary	dt. Bedeutung	English phrase	syn/opp
affluent	wohlhabend, reich	affluent people are very rich and have a high standard of living	= rich, wealthy, prosperous
(to) balance	ausgleichen, bilanzieren	to equal or equalise in weight, number, or proportion	
balance of payments	Zahlungsbilanz	The British balance of payments shows a surplus.	
bankrupt	bankrott, zahlungsunfähig	Many tradesmen go bankrupt because the building contractors don't pay their bills.	
bankruptcy	Bankrott	Due to the rise in the oil price many companies were facing bankruptcy.	
black economy	Schattenwirtschaft	work which is not official but which people do to avoid paying taxes	= twilight economy, hidden economy
boom	Hochkonjunktur	period of economic prosperity	
break-even point	Gewinnschwelle, Kostendeckungspunkt	Airliners have a break-even point at a load of about 70% of capacity.	
budget	Etat, öffentlicher Haushalt	The government tries to balance the budget.	
commerce	Handel, Verkehr	Commerce between England and the USA has grown steadily.	= business, trade

Economy

vocabulary	dt. Bedeutung	English phrase	syn/opp
commodity	*Ware*	a raw material or primary agricultural product that can be bought and sold, such as copper or coffee	
competitive	*konkurrenzfähig, wettbewerbsfähig*	The manager believed that the price for the new computer monitor was very competitive.	
competitor	*Konkurrent*in, Wettbewerber*in*	"We must try to be better than our foreign competitor."	= rival; ≠ partner
depression	*Wirtschaftskrise*	a long and severe recession in an economy (e.g. the Great Depression of 1929)	≠ boom
(to) evaluate	*auswerten, bewerten, beurteilen*	The chairman began to evaluate the financial situation of the company.	= to assess, to judge
expenses [Pl.]	*Spesen, Geldausgaben*	The representative's travelling expenses are very high this month.	= expenditure
free enterprise	*freies Unternehmertum*	an economic system in which private business operates without interference of the state	
friendly takeover	*freundliche Übernahme*	when a company buys another firm with the approval of that firm	≠ hostile takeover
globalisation	*Globalisierung*	a worldwide market without any barriers, with free flow of capital, products and services	
(to) go public	*an die Börse gehen*	Ten years after launch the cloud provider went public on the stock exchange.	

vocabulary	dt. Bedeutung	English phrase	syn/opp
gross domestic product (GDP)	Bruttoinlandsprodukt	the total value of goods produced and services provided by a country during one year	
gross national product (GNP)	Bruttosozialprodukt	The GNP is the volume of goods and services produced by the workforce of a country.	
hostile takeover	feindliche Übernahme	when a company buys another firm against the expressed wishes of that firm	≠ friendly takeover
Inland Revenue [UK]	Finanzamt	the department responsible for the collection of taxes	= finance authority
lean manufacturing	schlanke Produktion	Lean manufacturing means to limit production to just enough output to satisfy demand.	
limited company (ltd)	Gesellschaft mit beschränkter Haftung (GmbH)	London's renowned department store Harrods Ltd. was founded as a grocery store in 1849.	
(to be) listed on the stock exchange	an der Börse notiert (sein)	Facebook shares have been listed on the stock exchange since 2012.	
magnitude	Größe, Ausmaß	The Great Depression in the 1930s was of a much greater magnitude than any other business downturn.	= size, scope, extent, dimension
management buy-out (MBO)	Ankauf eines Unternehmens durch Mitglieder der Firma	The company was only able to stay in business after an MBO.	

vocabulary	dt. Bedeutung	English phrase	syn/opp
manufactured goods	*Fertigwaren*	More money is earned by the sale of manufactured goods than with the sale of primary products.	= finished products
merger **(to) merge**	*Fusion* *fusionieren*	Recent mergers in the communication sector have reduced the number of providers.	
monetary	*Geld-, Währungs-*	One of the aims of the Bank of England's monetary policy is to keep inflation low.	
(to) nationalise	*verstaatlichen*	to transfer (a major branch of industry or commerce) from private to state ownership or control, e. g. the railways	≠ to privatise
overheads	*laufende Geschäftskosten, Gemeinkosten*	business expenses (such as rent, insurance, or heating)	
parent company	*Muttergesellschaft*	The new firm already accounts for 15 % of its parent company's income.	
plentiful	*reichlich*	The successes of American business and industry are based on plentiful resources, the geographical size of the country and its population.	≠ scarce
prosperity	*Wohlstand, Gedeihen*	"We are now entering a period of prosperity for all!"	= wealth, economic well-being, affluence ≠ poverty, misery

Economy

vocabulary	dt. Bedeutung	English phrase	syn/opp
public limited company (plc)	Aktiengesellschaft (AG)	Pearson plc, a multinational publishing and education company, has its headquarters in London.	= corporation [US]
purchasing power	Kaufkraft	Different currencies have different purchasing power both in international trade and at home.	
recession	Rezession, Konjunkturrückgang	a period, shorter than a depression, during which there is a decline in economic trade and prosperity	= slump, stagnation
schedule	Zeit-/Fahrplan	The assistant worked out a schedule for the manager's trip to Japan.	= timetable, programme, plan
service industry	Dienstleistungssektor	More jobs will be created in the service industry.	
share	Aktie	After the crash at the stock exchange people hesitated to buy shares again.	
shareholder	Aktionär*in	sb who owns a share in property or in a company	
state-owned company	Staatsunternehmen	a company in the hands and under control of the state	
stocks	Aktien, Wertpapiere	capital of a company, usually divided into shares	
subsidiary	Tochter (-unternehmen)	a firm controlled by a holding company	
(to) subsidise	subventionieren, bezuschussen	In some developing countries governments subsidise basic foods.	
supplier	Lieferant*in	a person selling or making available sth that is needed	

vocabulary	dt. Bedeutung	English phrase	syn/opp
supply and demand	*Angebot und Nachfrage*	Supply and demand determine the price of a product.	
tight	*streng; dicht*	The government followed a tight monetary policy to control inflation.	= strict, tough, hard
(to) undercut sb	*jdn. im Preis unterbieten*	to offer goods or services at a lower price than a competitor	

2   Managing finances

vocabulary	dt. Bedeutung	English phrase	syn/opp
account	*Konto*	I'd like to open an account, please.	
account holder	*Kontoinhaber*in*	The bank was accused of selling personal details of account holders to other firms.	
application form	*Antragsformular*	I will complete the application form for you.	
ATM (automated teller machine) [US]	*Geldautomat*	At most banks there is an ATM in the lobby.	
bank charges	*Kontoführungsgebühren*	Bank charges have gone up a lot lately.	
bank clerk	*Bankangestellte*r*	I'm working as a bank clerk with the NatWest in Bromley.	
bank manager	*Bankdirektor*in, Filialleiter*in*	Could I speak to the bank manager, please?	

Economy

vocabulary	dt. Bedeutung	English phrase	syn/opp
beneficiary	Begünstigte*r, Nutznießer*in	The beneficiary is the person who receives the money from a trust or an insurance policy.	
BIC (bank identifier code)	Bankleitzahl	For money transfers you must know the recipient's IBAN and BIC.	
bill	[AE] Banknote	I haven't got any $ 20 bills on me.	
	[BE] Rechnung	Can I have the bill, please?	
branch	Filiale, Zweigstelle	a local office of a large business or bank	
(to) cancel	kündigen, auflösen	A standing order runs until you cancel it.	= to annul
cash dispenser [UK]	Geldautomat	You can operate the cash dispenser with your debit card.	= cash point [UK], cash machine, ATM
cash on delivery (COD)	per Nachnahme	The merchandise you ordered must be paid cash on delivery.	
cashier	Kassierer*in	a person handling money in a bank or shop	= teller [US]
charge	Gebühr	The bank offers: no charge on overdrafts of up to £ 100.	= fee
checking account [US]	Girokonto ohne Dispositionskredit	In the USA normal current accounts are known as checking accounts.	= current account [UK]
(to) credit	gutschreiben	On a German statement an "H" next to the amount means that the sum was credited to you.	
credit balance	Guthaben	The bank pays 0.5 % on credit balances of 10,000 euros and over.	

vocabulary	dt. Bedeutung	English phrase	syn/opp
credit limit	Kreditrahmen, Dispositionskredit	The bank informs you of your credit limit.	
creditor	Gläubiger*in	a person or company to whom you owe money	≠ debtor
current account	Girokonto, Kontokorrentkonto	I keep my current account with Barclays Bank.	
(to) debit	belasten, abbuchen	On a German statement an "S" next to the amount means that the sum was debited from you.	
debit balance	Sollsaldo	Interest must be paid on any debit balance that your account shows.	
debit card	Bankkarte	Do you prefer paying cash or by debit card?	= bank card
debit entry	Sollbuchung	On a German statement a debit entry is marked with an "S".	
debtor	Schuldner*in	sb who owes money	
direct debit authorisation	Einzugsermächtigung	With a direct debit authorisation you authorise sb to debit your account.	
direct debiting	Einzugs-, Abbuchungs-, Lastschriftverfahren	Can you explain how direct debiting works?	
(to) disclose	bekannt geben, verraten	You mustn't disclose your PIN to anyone!	= to reveal ≠ to conceal, to hide
exchange rate	Wechselkurs	The exchange rate tells you how much you have to pay to buy a foreign currency.	

Economy

vocabulary	dt. Bedeutung	English phrase	syn/opp
foreign exchange	*Devisen*	Meryl works in the foreign exchange department of the Hong Kong and Shanghai Banking Corporation.	
(to) grant a credit	*einen Kredit gewähren*	Banks grant credits to their customers.	= to give
IBAN (international bank account number)	*internationale Bankkontonummer*	For money transfers you must know the recipient's IBAN and BIC.	
(to) insert	*(Karte bei Automaten) einführen*	Please insert your card into the slot.	
interest [Sg.]	*Zins(en)*	Investors want their money to earn interest.	
investor	*(Geld-)Anleger*in*	Banks deal in securities for investors.	
joint account	*gemeinsames Konto*	My wife and I have a joint account.	
letter of credit	*Kreditbrief, Akkreditiv*	authorisation made by a buyer to his/her agent (usually a bank) to make payment to a seller	
loan	*Darlehen, Kredit*	money (borrowed from a bank) for which you have to pay interest	= credit
means of payment	*Zahlungsmittel*	The most popular means of payment in the USA is by credit card.	
mortgage	*Hypothek, Verpfändung*	The Johnsons found it hard to repay their mortgage.	
non-cash	*bargeldlos*	Most firms prefer non-cash payment.	

vocabulary	dt. Bedeutung	English phrase	syn/opp
online banking	Internet-, Onlinebanking	Banks inform customers of the advantages of online banking.	= electronic/Internet banking
overdraft	Kontoüberziehung, Kontokorrentkredit, Dispositionskredit	Banks lend money to their customers by granting overdrafts.	
(to) overdraw	sein Konto überziehen	Be careful not to overdraw your account too much.	
PIN (personal identification number)	persönliche Geheimzahl	a number given to a bank customer so that he/she can use the cash machine	
power of attorney	Vollmacht	the authority to act in your name	
(to) raise capital	Kapital aufbringen	Banks help companies to raise capital for financing.	= to raise money
reminder	Mahnung	If customers don't pay their debts, firms have to send off one or two reminders.	
(to) retain	zurückbehalten, einziehen	Cash dispensers retain cards if an incorrect PIN has been punched three consecutive times.	
revenue	Einnahmen, Erlös	money received or gained	= income
savings account	Sparkonto	You can earn more interest if you keep your money in a savings account.	
securities [Pl.]	Wertpapiere, Effekten	Banks deal in securities for investors.	
specimen signature	Unterschriftsprobe	Please give us a specimen signature on this form.	
standing order	Dauerauftrag	Most people pay their rent by standing order.	

vocabulary	dt. Bedeutung	English phrase	syn/opp
statement	(Konto-)Auszug	The bank advises its customers to check their bank statements carefully.	
TAN (transaction authentication number)	TAN (Transaktionsnummer)	You need a mobile TAN for every transaction when doing online banking.	
(to) transfer	überweisen	Firms such as PayPal transfer money securely through the Internet.	
(to) withdraw	(Geld) abheben	to take out money of an account	
withdrawal	Abhebung	You should inform your bank in advance if you wish to make a large cash withdrawal.	

3 Consumer

vocabulary	dt. Bedeutung	English phrase	syn/opp
bargain	Schnäppchen, Angebot, (gutes) Geschäft	In the winter sale Mrs Appleton got a real bargain: she bought a coat which was reduced to £ 56.	
best-before-date	Mindesthaltbarkeitsdatum	McVitie's chocolate biscuits. Best before 28th November.	
branded goods [Pl.]	Markenartikel	goods produced by well-known manufacturers which have the manufacturers' label on them	≠ no-name product
(to) compel	zwingen, verpflichten	No manufacturer is compelled to give a guarantee.	= to oblige, to force

vocabulary	dt. Bedeutung	English phrase	syn/opp
consumer goods [Pl.]	Verbrauchsgüter, Konsumgüter	British standards for consumer goods are rather high.	
consumer guidance	Verbraucherberatung	Readers get plenty of consumer guidance in most newspapers and magazines.	
consumer protection	Verbraucherschutz	Parliament has seen to it that the new law guarantees better consumer protection.	
customer complaint	Kundenbeschwerde, Reklamation	Companies should take customer complaints seriously.	
customer-friendly	kundenfreundlich	The new shop is really customer-friendly – they offer great service there.	
customer friendliness	Kundenfreundlichkeit		
dealer	Händler*in	a person or business that buys and sells goods	= merchant, business person
(to) depreciate	gering schätzen	You shouldn't depreciate the information offered in public health warnings!	= to devalue, to think little of; ≠ to appreciate
discernible	erkennbar	High quality products are not always easily discernible.	= recognizable, noticeable
discount	Rabatt	a reduction in the usual price	= rebate, reduction
(to) dispatch	absenden, abfertigen	We shall dispatch the goods you ordered tomorrow.	= to send off
fee	Gebühr, (Honorar-)Zahlung	The 'Stiftung Warentest' does not accept fees from manufacturers.	= payment

vocabulary	dt. Bedeutung	English phrase	syn/opp
inaccurate	*nicht zutreffend, falsch, ungenau*	The description on the label of these jeans is inaccurate.	= false, wrong, inexact
irritation	*Verärgerung, Gereiztheit*	The lack of good service in department stores caused some irritation.	= anger
merchandise	*Handelsware*	goods to be bought and sold	
non-profit	*gemeinnützig*	The German 'Stiftung Warentest' is a non-profit organisation.	
purchase	*Kauf, Erwerb*	If you ask for a refund, we need to know the exact date of purchase.	= buy, buying
range	*Sortiment, Kollektion*	The little corner shop sells only a limited range of foodstuffs.	= assortment
refund	*Rückzahlung, Rückerstattung*	Without a receipt we cannot guarantee a refund.	
reply coupon	*Antwortschein, Antwortcoupon*	a voucher *(Bon)* used for prepaying the postage	
response	*Erwiderung, Reaktion, Antwort*	As an immediate response the firm reduced the price of its product by 20 %.	= reply, answer
retail price	*Einzelhandelspreis*	the price of a product in the shops	
seal	*Siegel, Bestätigung*	A manufacturer's private seal informs the consumer about the quality of the product.	= signet
sell-by date	*Haltbarkeitsdatum*	The sell-by date informs the customer about the freshness of the product.	

vocabulary	dt. Bedeutung	English phrase	syn/opp
(to) soar	in die Höhe schnellen, rapide steigen	As raw materials became more expensive, consumer prices soared.	= to rise, to rocket
standard	Maßstab, Norm	Marks and Spencer's standard for the quality of fresh foods is very high.	= norm
stock	Vorrat, Warenbestand, Warenlager	We keep more than 35,000 books in stock.	
transgression	Übertretung, Vergehen gegen	Any transgression of the British Retail Trade Standards will be prosecuted.	= violation, offence against
trustworthy	vertrauenswürdig	Customers want to do business with a company which is trustworthy.	= honest, dependable
variety	Vielfalt, Mannigfaltigkeit	Consumers today have a variety of products to choose from.	= diversity
VAT (value added tax)	Mehrwertsteuer	Our prices include VAT and postage.	
wasteful	verschwenderisch, kostspielig	We must do something against the wasteful use of scarce resources.	= extravagant
(to) wrap	(in Papier) einwickeln	Shall I wrap this book as a present, madam?	

4 Advertising

vocabulary	dt. Bedeutung	English phrase	syn/opp
ad	*Anzeige*	Many big companies use Google ads to appear first in an online search.	= advert, advertisement
(to) advertise	*inserieren, werben*		
advertising campaign	*Werbekampagne*	The chairman favours the development of a new advertising campaign.	
advertising revenue	*Werbeeinnahmen*	money earned through advertising	
brand	*Marke, Markenbezeichnung*	a product manufactured by a particular company under a particular name	
brand loyalty	*Markentreue*	buying from the same manufacturer	
cash cow	*Goldesel, umsatzstarkes Produkt*	a product which has been very profitable for a long time	
commercial	*Werbesendung, -spot,*	I like watching commercials on YouTube, because some of them are quite funny.	
(to) conceal	*verbergen, verstecken, verheimlichen*	Don't try to conceal the whole truth from me.	= to hide
concealed advertising	*Schleichwerbung*	Videos and online posts by "influencers" can contain concealed advertising.	
(to) conceive	*sich vorstellen, ausdenken, planen, ersinnen*	It's very hard to conceive a better marketing policy for our new product.	= to contrive, to devise
(to) deceive	*trügen, täuschen*	Bright and colourful packages sometimes deceive the consumers.	= to cheat, to fool, to mislead, to delude

vocabulary	dt. Bedeutung	English phrase	syn/opp
distribution	Vertrieb	Our company is using different distribution channels.	
distributor	Händler, Vertreiber	An important distributor will always try to sell his own brand of goods.	= dealer, trader
(to) exhibit (at a trade fair) exhibitor	ausstellen (auf einer Messe) Aussteller*in	to show goods to the public	
freebie	Zugabe, Werbegeschenk	sth given away without asking money for it	
hard sell	aggressive Verkaufstaktik	aggressive advertising (often involves applying psychological pressure)	= high pressure selling ≠ soft sell
(to) ignite	an-, entzünden, entfachen	A clever commercial will always ignite a spark in the consumer's mind.	= to arouse the interest
(to) launch	in den Markt einführen, präsentieren	The new electric car is to be launched in the US next month.	
loss leader	Lockvogelangebot	a product which is sold at a loss in order to draw customers	
mail shot	Direktwerbung (per Post)	direct advertising by post	
market leader	Marktführer	Microsoft is the market leader in office computer programmes.	
market research	Marktforschung	Firms invest a lot of money in market research.	
market share	Marktanteil	percentage of the market for a product or service that a company supplies	

Economy

vocabulary	dt. Bedeutung	English phrase	syn/opp
market survey	Marktuntersuchung	"How much would you pay for our product?" is a good question for a market survey.	= market research
(to) mislead	irreführen, betrügen	If you want loyal customers, don't ever mislead them.	= to cheat, to trick
niche	Nische	a specialised but profitable corner of the market	
online advertising	Werbung im Internet	Online advertising has become increasingly popular because of its relatively wide reach.	= digital advertising
package	Verpackung	The artist M. F. Ginger designed a new package for McCall's new brand of cornflakes.	
performance	Leistung	All our test customers were happy with the performance of the new steam iron.	
potential	eventuell, möglich	The company's aim is to find out what colour potential customers would prefer.	
preference	Vorliebe, Präferenz	Do you have a preference for a certain brand?	
(to) promote promotion	fördern, steigern, werben für Werbeaktion	With frequent TV appearances the pop star managed to promote sales of his latest album.	
(to) prosecute	gerichtlich verfolgen	The Retail Trade Association will prosecute any false trade descriptions.	

vocabulary	dt. Bedeutung	English phrase	syn/opp
questionnaire	Fragebogen	a set of written questions to find out people's opinions about a product	
sales figures	Verkaufszahlen	Sales figures have been up by 25 %.	
sales representative	Vertreter*in	a person travelling around to inform potential customers about his/her firm's product range	= sales rep
sample	Muster	a small part or quantity of a product to show the customer what the complete article is like	
search engine marketing (SEM)	Suchmaschinenmarketing	Internet marketing to increase the visibility of websites on search engine result pages	
slogan	Werbespruch	The dairy industry was very successful with the slogan "Drink a pint 'a milk a day!"	
soft sell	weiche Verkaufstaktik	the use of suggestion or gentle persuasion in selling	≠ hard sell
subtle	fein, subtil	Advertising has definitely become more subtle.	≠ blatant, crude
(to) target	abzielen auf, anvisieren	Businesses spend large amounts of money targeting children with ads.	
target group	Zielgruppe	Young people have always been a preferred target group of advertisers.	
video advertising	Videowerbung	Video advertising on YouTube has become a profitable source of income for the site's owner Google.	

The world of work

1 Working life

vocabulary	dt. Bedeutung	English phrase	syn/opp
accountant	Steuerberater*in, Buchhalter*in	a person who keeps or inspects the financial accounts of a company	
apprentice apprenticeship	Lehrling, Auszubildende*r Lehrzeit, Lehre	If you want to learn a trade properly, you must start as an apprentice.	
(to) assemble	montieren, zusammensetzen	In that huge building over there they assemble the latest model of the Airbus.	= to put together, to build
blue-collar worker	Arbeiter*in	someone who does manual work	≠ white-collar worker
board of directors	Verwaltungsrat, Aufsichtsrat	The members of the board of directors will meet the trade union representatives on Monday.	= supervisory board, administrative board
career	Laufbahn, Beruf	She started her career as a teacher of English.	= vocation, profession, calling
careers officer	Berufsberater*in	A careers officer came to school to inform school-leavers about their job prospects.	
career opportunities	Berufschancen	job chances	
CEO (chief executive officer)	Generaldirektor*in, Geschäftsführer*in	person responsible for a firm's business transactions	

The world of work

vocabulary	dt. Bedeutung	English phrase	syn/opp
(to) clock in	einstempeln	It is illegal to clock in for a friend who hasn't arrived for work yet.	≠ to clock out
commission	Provision	money paid to an agent or employee for performing a service	
consultant	Berater*in	a person who provides expert advice	
conveyor belt	Montageband, Fließband	Tom Birch stands at a conveyor belt all day.	= assembly line
craftsman/ craftswoman	(gelernte*r) Handwerker*in	Mr Tylor is an excellent craftsman: he really knows how to make beautiful chairs.	= craftsperson
craftsmanship	Kunstfertigkeit		
deduction (to) deduct	Abzug abziehen	an amount taken away from a sum of money	≠ addition
(to) dismiss	entlassen	I cannot believe that the factory wants to dismiss more than 500 people from their jobs!	= to discharge, to sack, to fire
dole (to) be on the dole	Arbeitslosengeld Arbeitslosengeld bekommen, stempeln gehen	Fred Compton has been on the dole for over eight months.	
employee	Angestellte*r, Arbeitnehmer*in	This company has more than 4,600 employees.	
employer	Arbeitgeber	The central organisation of British employers is called Confederation of British Industry.	
(to) enter a career	eine Laufbahn einschlagen	More women are encouraged to enter a career in engineering.	

The world of work

vocabulary	dt. Bedeutung	English phrase	syn/opp
(to) found	*gründen*	IBM (International Business Machines Corporation) was founded in 1911.	= to establish, to start, to set up
freelancer	*Freiberufler*in*	a person who works without a long-term commitment to any one employer	
human resources	*Arbeitskräfte*	the personnel of a business or organisation	= staff
HR (Human Resources)	*Personalabteilung*	HR managers are responsible for recruiting and interviewing job applicants.	
job centre	*Arbeitsamt*	Every morning there is a long queue of job seekers outside the job centre.	= labor office [US], labour exchange
jobseeker	*Arbeitssuchende*r, Arbeitslose*r*	A job seeker can only turn down a job with a very good reason.	
jobseeker's allowance	*Arbeitslosengeld, Arbeitslosenhilfe*	Jobseeker's allowance is only paid to people who keep looking for a job.	
labour	*Arbeit, Arbeitskräfte*	Many firms experience difficulty in recruiting skilled labour.	
labour exchange	*Arbeitsamt*	Every morning Gerry goes down to the labour exchange to find out if there are any suitable jobs going.	= job centre, labor office [US]
lay-off	*vorübergehende Entlassung*	Many managers feared that increased competition would cause lay-offs.	
(to) lay sb off	*jdn. entlassen*	When the new robot was installed twenty workers were laid off.	

vocabulary	dt. Bedeutung	English phrase	syn/opp
livelihood	*Auskommen, Lebensunterhalt, Unterhalt*	Sam Withby earns his livelihood by teaching.	= living
loyalty	*Treue*	I am convinced of your loyalty to the company.	= faithfulness, fidelity
(to) make a living	*seinen Lebensunterhalt verdienen*	to earn money to live on	
manpower [Pl.]	*Arbeitskräfte*	As the new product sold rather well, the firm decided to increase manpower in the production plant.	= workforce, labour force
manual labour	*körperliche Arbeit, Handarbeit*	Robots have taken over some dangerous manual labour.	
minimum wage	*Mindestlohn*	John earns little more than the minimum wage.	
national insurance contributions	*Beiträge zur Sozialversicherung*	National insurance contributions have gone up.	= social security contributions
notice (to) give notice	*Kündigung kündigen*	In order to save costs, the firm had to give notice to 250 employees.	
without notice	*fristlos*	As he had stolen some tools from the shop floor, Angus McDowell was dismissed without notice.	
part-timer	*Teilzeitkraft, Teilzeitbeschäftigte*r*	Call centres are often staffed by part-timers.	
personnel	*Personal, Belegschaft*	The personnel shortage in hospitals and nursing homes is alarming.	= staff, workforce

The world of work

vocabulary	dt. Bedeutung	English phrase	syn/opp
plant	*Anlage, Werk*	German firms helped to build a chemical plant in Asia.	= works, factory, mill
profession	*(akademischer) Beruf*	For a profession (e. g. lawyer, doctor, teacher), an advanced education and a special training are required.	
(to) enter a profession	*einen Beruf ergreifen*		
(to) promote promotion	*jdn. befördern Beförderung*	The board of directors has decided to promote Alwyn Reeves to deputy staff manager.	
(to) qualify	*sich eignen*	In order to qualify for the job, you will need more experience.	= be suited for
(to) recruit	*jdn. einstellen*	to enrol sb as a worker; to take on people as workers	= to enrol, to hire
redundancy payment	*Abfindung*	Most employees who lost their jobs received redundancy payments.	
requirement	*Anforderung, Voraussetzung*	The most important job requirements include ability to work in a team, flexibility and experience.	
(to) retire	*in Pension gehen, in Rente gehen, sich pensionieren lassen*	Harry can hardly wait till he's 62, because then he wants to retire and work in his garden all day long.	
revenue	*Einkünfte*	the total income	
royalties	*Tantiemen, Honorar*	the sum of money which is paid, e. g. to an author	
sack	*Rausschmiss, Entlassung*	The manager was sick and tired of Brian being late almost every day, so he gave him the sack.	
(to) sack	*rausschmeißen*		

The world of work

vocabulary	dt. Bedeutung	English phrase	syn/opp
salary	*Gehalt*	If you take this job, you can earn a salary of £ 24,900 a year.	
self-employed	*selbstständig*	earning income directly from one's own business	
semi-skilled worker	*angelernte Arbeitskraft*	a person who has less training in a job than a skilled labourer	
senior manager	*leitende*r Angestellte*r*	a manager holding a higher and more important position in a company	
shift	*Schicht*	For most of his life William Peel has been working night shift.	
skill shortage	*Fachkräftemangel*	shortage of trained and experienced staff	
skilled worker	*Facharbeiter*in*	Skilled workers have greater chances of finding the type of job they want.	
staff	*Belegschaft*	The company employs a staff of 287.	= workforce
staff manager	*Personalchef*in*	I'd like to talk to the staff manager about my complaint, please.	= manager of personnel, HR manager
temporary worker	*Zeitarbeiter*in, Leiharbeiter*in*	To save costs, the firm employs more temporary workers than full-time staff.	= contract worker, agency worker
time clock	*Stechuhr, Zeituhr, Stempeluhr*	A time clock is used to record and manage staff attendance, punctuality and overtime.	
trainee	*Praktikant*in, in der Ausbildung Stehende*r*	Richard works as a trainee reporter for *The Daily Telegraph*.	

The world of work **109**

vocabulary	dt. Bedeutung	English phrase	syn/opp
unemployed	*arbeitslos*	Ralph has been unemployed for two years.	= jobless, out of work
unemployment benefit	*Arbeitslosengeld*	As Jennifer has lost her job, she now draws unemployment benefit.	= unemployment funds
unskilled worker	*ungelernte Arbeitskraft*	sb who has no training	≠ skilled
vacancy	*freie/offene Stelle*	Martin, who's a trained carpenter, is looking for a vacancy in his area.	= job
virtually	*praktisch, eigentlich*	Virtually all the net growth in employment in recent years has come from part-time jobs.	= practically, nearly
white-collar worker	*(Büro-)Angestellte*r*	sb who works in an office or a bank	= clerk
workforce	*Belegschaft*	Our company employs a mixed-age workforce.	= staff, personnel, human resources
workshop	*Werkstatt*	We have to send the broken machine to the workshop.	

2 Work-life balance, diversity and compliance

vocabulary	dt. Bedeutung	English phrase	syn/opp
alienation	*Entfremdung*	Many workers who have to carry out boring routine work suffer from job alienation.	
bore-out	*Bore-Out(-Syndrom), chronische Unterforderung*	To save himself from bore-out, Jeff left his routine 9-to-5 office job and joined the fire brigade.	

vocabulary	dt. Bedeutung	English phrase	syn/opp
burn-out	Burnout(-Syndrom), Ausgebranntsein	Burn-out syndrome is characterised by too much stress on the job leading to exhaustion and reduced satisfaction.	
career break	Unterbrechung der beruflichen Tätigkeit	People who take a career break to care for elderly family members need more financial help.	
code of conduct	Verhaltenskodex, Verhaltensgrundsätze	A code of conduct defines acceptable behaviour at work for the company's employees.	
code of ethics	Ethikkodex	A code of ethics sets out the company's values, ethics, objective and responsibilities.	
compliance	Compliance, regelgerechtes Verhalten	abiding by laws, regulations and ethical standards	
CWW (compressed work week)	komprimierte Arbeitswoche	A common type of CWW consists of four 10-hour days with every Friday off.	
diverse workforce	vielfältige Belegschaft	A diverse workforce is comprised of people of different ages, cultures, viewpoints and backgrounds.	
diversity	Diversität, Vielfalt	Companies that embrace diversity and inclusion are usually more innovative and successful.	

The world of work

vocabulary	dt. Bedeutung	English phrase	syn/opp
(to) downshift	*kürzer treten, das Arbeitspensum reduzieren, „einen Gang herunterschalten"*	Many working fathers would like to downshift from full-time work in order to have more time for their family.	
equal pay	*gleiche Bezahlung*	In the United States, equal pay has been the law since 1963.	
flexitime	*Gleitzeit, gleitende Arbeitszeit*	Employers are concerned that flexitime employees won't have enough time at the office to collaborate with co-workers.	= flexible working hours
gender pay gap	*Lohngefälle zwischen Männern und Frauen*	The gender pay gap is the difference between average hourly earnings for men and women.	
hot-desking	*Hotdesking (mehrere Beschäftigte teilen sich einen Büroarbeitsplatz)*	a flexible form of working where several temporary workers share a desk	
job sharing	*Jobsharing*	For some people job sharing is a good way to increase their flexibility and improve their work-life balance.	
low-wage job	*niedrig (schlecht) bezahlte Arbeit*	Unfortunately, taking care of sick or elderly people is still a low-wage job.	= low-paying job ≠ high-wage job
male-dominated	*von Männern beherrscht*	Many women find it hard to get to the top in a male-dominated business world.	≠ female-dominated
(to) outperform	*an Leistung übertreffen*	Ethan always tries to outperform his colleagues.	

vocabulary	dt. Bedeutung	English phrase	syn/opp
overtime	*Überstunden*	time worked over and above one's normal working hours	
part-time job	*Teilzeitarbeit*	Parents are often eager for part-time jobs that allow them to combine work with child-rearing.	≠ full-time job
promotion prospects	*Aufstiegschancen*	Further training increases your promotion prospects.	= career prospects
quota	*Anteil*	The quota of women on our company board is still too low.	= share, percentage
reputation	*Ruf, Ansehen*	Our company has a good reputation as an employer.	
sabbatical	*Sabbatjahr, längerer Sonderurlaub*	Many people use a sabbatical to travel, do social work or pursue their passions.	
self-assertion	*Selbstbehauptung, Durchsetzungsvermögen*	Some people think that self-assertion is necessary for professional success.	
self-realisation	*Selbstverwirklichung*	Most people choose a profession in the hope of personal and economic self-realisation.	
(to) track	*(nach-)verfolgen*	Amazon has patented a wristband that tracks the hand movements of warehouse workers.	
two-earner household	*Haushalt, in dem zwei verdienen*	Britain has more two-earner households than before, but still too many no-earner households.	

The world of work **113**

vocabulary	dt. Bedeutung	English phrase	syn/opp
worker turnover	Fluktuation, Personalwechsel	The growing problem of job stress also results in increasing worker turnover.	
work-life balance	Work-Life-Balance, Vereinbarkeit von Beruf und Privatleben	Flexible working hours are one way to maintain a work-life balance.	≠ work-life imbalance

3 Trade unions

vocabulary	dt. Bedeutung	English phrase	syn/opp
(to be) anxious	auf etw. bedacht (sein)	The employers are anxious to reach a compromise with the workers who are on strike.	= keen, eager
blackleg	Streikbrecher*in	A blackleg usually has to suffer a lot of insults from workers who are out on strike.	= strike breaker
(to) call a strike	einen Streik ausrufen	The General Workers' Union will probably call a strike.	
collective bargaining [Pl.]	Tarifverhandlungen	The employers and the unions have entered into collective bargaining.	
consensus	Übereinstimmung	the opinion of all or most of the people consulted	= agreement, consent
industrial action	Streik	The union members voted against industrial action.	
(to) lock out	aussperren	The managers decide today whether they will lock out the workers who are on strike.	

The world of work

vocabulary	dt. Bedeutung	English phrase	syn/opp
negotiation	*Verhandlung*	If negotiations fail, the printers will go on strike and there won't be any newspapers tomorrow.	= talks
picket	*Streikposten, Streikwache*	The printers' union placed pickets at the factory gates to make sure that no worker would break the strike.	
shop steward	*gewerkschaftliche Vertrauensperson*	In our printing plant, Joe Cooper is the shop steward of the printers' union.	
strike	*Streik*	If the employers don't pay us more, there will be a strike soon.	= walkout
strike vote	*Urabstimmung*	The union must carry out a strike vote among its members before it can call a strike.	
trade union	*Gewerkschaft*	In the 19th century the first trade union was formed.	= labor union [US]
upheaval	*Umwälzung, Aufruhr*	The Industrial Revolution caused a great upheaval in England's social structure.	= upturn
wildcat strike	*wilder (illegaler) Streik*	If the union doesn't carry out a vote before a strike, the strike is illegal: it's a wildcat strike.	
working conditions	*Arbeitsbedingungen*	The trade unions fight for better working conditions.	

Agriculture and developing countries

1 Agriculture

vocabulary	dt. Bedeutung	English phrase	syn/opp
abundant	*reichlich*	The fertile areas of the US have abundant rainfall.	= plentiful
agriculture	*Landwirtschaft*	In the USA, agriculture has always played a major role in the economy.	= farming
animal welfare	*Tierschutz, Tierwohl*	Animal welfare on farms should be improved.	= protection of animals
(to) apply to	*an-, verwenden*	Farmers should apply fewer pesticides to their crops.	
arable farming	*Ackerbau*	The soil in the Great Lakes area is less suited to arable farming.	
chemical-free farming	*biologische Landwirtschaft*	Chemical-free farming can be just as productive as traditional methods of agriculture.	= alternative farming, non-chemical farming
corn [AE]	*Mais*	The Corn Belt stretches from the Allegheny Mountains to Missouri.	= maize [BE]
crop	*Feldfrucht, Gesamternte*	plants that are grown in large quantities for food	
dairy belt	*Milchwirtschaftsgürtel (USA)*	The Dairy Belt extends through New England and the Great Lakes area.	
dairy farming	*Milchwirtschaft, Milchviehhaltung*	Dairy farming increasingly relies on new technologies such as milking robots.	

115

Agriculture and developing countries

vocabulary	dt. Bedeutung	English phrase	syn/opp
dairy produce	Milch-, Molkereiprodukte	foods that are made from milk	
(to) devastate	vernichten, verwüsten	Heavy storms and floods devastated much of the country's fertile land.	= to ruin, to destroy
(to) exhaust	erschöpfen, auslaugen	Inefficient farming methods have exhausted the soil.	
factory farm factory farming	Massentierhaltungsbetrieb Massentierhaltung	Animal rights activists criticise the cruel treatment of animals on factory farms.	
fertile fertility	fruchtbar Fruchtbarkeit	producing or bearing fruit in great quantities	≠ infertile, barren
fertiliser	Dünger, Düngemittel	Fertilisers are used to revitalise the soil.	
food safety	Lebensmittelsicherheit	Public concern about food safety has increased since the arrival of genetically modified foods.	
GM (genetically modified)	gentechnisch verändert	GM soya is commonplace in the USA.	
grain	Korn(-art), Getreide(-art)	The rotation of corn with other grain keeps the soil fertile.	= cereal
granary	Kornkammer	a region producing large quantities of corn	
growing season	Wachstums-, Reifezeit	In the Great Lakes area the growing season is rather short.	
harvest	Ernte(-zeit)	time of year when the agricultural crops are gathered	
herbicide	Unkrautbekämpfungsmittel	a chemical needed to destroy weeds	

Agriculture and developing countries

vocabulary	dt. Bedeutung	English phrase	syn/opp
industrial farming	*industrielle Landwirtschaft*	Industrial farming aims at maximising output, often at the expense of animal welfare and the environment.	= intensive agriculture ≠ sustainable farming
level land	*Flachland*	The Corn Belt occupies the USA's largest continuous area of fertile level land.	
livestock	*Nutztier(e)*	animals raised on farms	
mixed farming	*Mischlandwirtschaft*	The Corn Belt has a genuine mixed farming system.	
moist	*feucht*	slightly or moderately wet	= damp, humid
nutrient	*Nährstoff*	Rotation of crops keeps nutrients in the soil naturally.	
organic farming	*biologische Landwirtschaft*	Organic farming has grown in importance.	= biological agriculture
pasture	*Weide(-fläche)*	land covered with grass	
pest	*Schädling*	an insect or other animal that attacks crops, food and livestock	
pesticide	*Schädlingsbekämpfungsmittel*	a substance used to destroy insects which harm plants	
primary product	*Rohstoff*	Peru sells primary products like minerals and cotton.	= raw material
produce	*(landwirtschaftl.) Erzeugnisse*	The farmer takes his produce to the market every Saturday.	
rotation	*Fruchtwechsel, Abwechslung*	The rotation of corn with other grains preserves the fertility of the soil.	
soil	*Boden*	Soil erosion is a serious problem.	= ground, earth

Agriculture and developing countries

vocabulary	dt. Bedeutung	English phrase	syn/opp
subsidy	*Subvention*	a sum of money to support farmers and promote a certain kind of agriculture	
surplus	*Überschuss*	Farmers should be discouraged from producing surpluses which they cannot market.	
weed	*Unkraut*	a wild plant which grows in a place where it is not wanted	
wheat	*Weizen*	The Wheat Belt is one of the world's chief granaries.	
yield	*Ertrag*	Farmers use fertilisers to increase yields.	

2 Problems in developing countries

vocabulary	dt. Bedeutung	English phrase	syn/opp
appalling	*entsetzlich, erschreckend*	People in the slums live in the most appalling conditions.	= shocking, dreadful, awful
(to) assess	*beurteilen, einschätzen, bewerten*	The most common way to assess a country's degree of development is by reference to its Gross National Product (GNP).	= to evaluate, to gauge
balance	*Gleichgewicht*	There should be a balance between a country's population and the available resources.	= equilibrium
(to) be devoted to	*ausgerichtet sein auf, gewidmet sein*	Much of the productive effort of developing countries is devoted to growing food.	= to be dedicated to

Agriculture and developing countries

vocabulary	dt. Bedeutung	English phrase	syn/opp
birth rate	*Geburtenrate*	the number of births for every hundred or every thousand persons	
calorie intake	*Kalorieneinnahme, -zufuhr*	Insufficient calorie intake can lead to malnutrition.	
(to) combat	*bekämpfen*	High beta-carotene oil is used to combat night blindness.	= to fight against
deficiency	*Mangel*	Vitamin A deficiency can cause night blindness.	= lack, shortage, inadequacy
desert	*Wüste*	Some developing countries are sun-baked deserts where crops do not grow.	
desperate	*verzweifelt, extrem*	The majority of people in developing countries live in desperate poverty.	
(to) deteriorate	*sich verschlechtern*	to become worse in condition	
diet	*Kost, Nahrung*	food that a person eats regularly	
disparity	*Ungleichheit*	unfair difference	= imbalance
drought	*Dürre*	a long period during which no rain falls	
family planning	*Familienplanung*	Family planning should be made freely available.	= birth control
fierce	*heftig, scharf, erbittert*	Fierce conflicts take place in some developing countries.	= intense, violent
hygiene	*Hygiene*	Hygiene standards in developing countries are often rather low.	
illiteracy	*Analphabetismus*	the inability to read or write	≠ literacy

Agriculture and developing countries

vocabulary	dt. Bedeutung	English phrase	syn/opp
indicator	*Anzeiger, Indikator*	The infant mortality rate is a social indicator for poverty in developing countries.	= gauge [ei]
industrialised nation	*Industrienation*	country with a strong economy, advanced infrastructure and high standard of living	
infant mortality	*Kindersterblichkeit*	the percentage of babies or young children who die	
life expectancy	*Lebenserwartung*	the length of time that people are normally likely to live	
malnutrition	*Unterernährung, schlechte Ernährung*	We have to fight hunger, disease, and malnutrition in developing countries.	
medical care	*medizinische Betreuung*	Medical care for people living in underdeveloped regions must be improved.	= medical attention
migrant	*Zuwanderer/ Zuwanderin*	a person who moves from one place to another, esp. to find work	
notion	*Vorstellung*	Internet access is an irrelevant notion in societies where even electricity is a luxury.	= idea, view, concept
nutritious	*nahrhaft*	Food intake in the form of grains, proteins, fruit and vegetables provides a nutritious diet.	= nourishing
overpopulation	*Überbevölkerung*	too many people living in one place	
pace	*Schritt, Tempo*	In developing countries, agriculture cannot keep pace with an exploding population.	= rate, speed

Agriculture and developing countries

vocabulary	dt. Bedeutung	English phrase	syn/opp
peasants [Pl.]	*Kleinbauern*	mostly poor people working on a small piece of land	
population growth	*Bevölkerungswachstum*	Population growth can be controlled by family planning.	
predominantly	*überwiegend*	In poor countries diets are predominantly starchy.	= largely, mainly
prevailing	*(vor-)herrschend, bestehend*	Rich countries should help to abolish the prevailing misery among the poorest people in the world.	= current, existing
(to) rank	*ordnen, einreihen, klassifizieren*	We often rank countries according to the average income earned per person.	= to rate
rate of mortality	*Sterberate*	The rate of mortality among children in developing countries is very high.	= death rate
(to) rely on	*sich verlassen auf*	People in Africa often can't rely on their governments to improve their situation.	= to trust, to count on
resources	*Ressourcen, Bodenschätze*	manpower and raw materials that a country possesses and can use	= assets
rural	*ländlich*	It is often very difficult for people living in rural areas to access healthcare.	≠ urban
scarce	*knapp, spärlich*	Food supplies are scarce and too many people die of hunger each year.	= rare
sewage	*Abwasser*	There is no sewage system in the slums; that's why often cholera and typhoid break out.	= waste water
shanty town	*Barackensiedlung, -stadt*	collection of rough huts in slum areas	

vocabulary	dt. Bedeutung	English phrase	syn/opp
starchy	*stärkehaltig*	Starchy diets do not provide enough protein.	
starvation	*Hunger*	Every day thousands of people die of starvation.	= famine, hunger
subsistence	*(Lebens-)Unterhalt*	Some poor peasants hardly produce enough food for their own subsistence.	
(to) supplement	*ergänzen*	It may be necessary to supplement one's diet with vitamins in order to avoid a deficiency.	
(to) surmount	*(eine Herausforderung/ein Problem) meistern*	to overcome a difficulty or an obstacle	
underfed	*unterernährt*	Many children in war-torn countries are underfed.	= undernourished
unmet need	*ungedeckter Bedarf*	International help must be increased to meet the unmet needs for population programmes.	
urgency	*Dringlichkeit*	In developing countries we are confronted with the urgency to fight hunger, disease, and malnutrition.	
vegetables	*Gemüse*	plants such as cabbages, potatoes and onions	
vicious circle	*Teufelskreis*	We must break the vicious circle between poverty and the rapid population growth.	
widespread	*weit verbreitet*	In the poor countries there are widespread deficiencies of proteins and essential vitamins.	= general

Environment

1 The world around us

vocabulary	dt. Bedeutung	English phrase	syn/opp
balance	*Gleichgewicht*	Species of plants or animals become extinct when human beings upset the balance of nature.	= equilibrium
biosphere	*Biosphäre, Lebensraum*	Our biosphere is in a state of delicate balance.	
climate	*Klima*	the regular pattern of weather conditions in a certain area	
delicate	*empfindlich*	The earth's biosphere is in a state of delicate balance.	= fragile
drought	*Dürre*	a long period of dry weather; lack of rain	≠ flood
ecology	*Ökologie*	the study of the relationship of plants and animals to their physical and biological environment	
environment	*Umwelt*	the natural world in which people, animals and plants live	= surroundings
environmental studies	*Umweltforschung*	Environmental studies show us how we can save our planet.	
environmentalist	*Umweltschützer*in*	Environmentalists warn us of the depletion of the ozone layer.	
environmentally aware	*umweltbewusst*	The number of environmentally aware shoppers is increasing.	

Environment

vocabulary	dt. Bedeutung	English phrase	syn/opp
equilibrium	*Gleichgewicht*	Too many factories will destroy the ecological equilibrium of the area.	= balance ≠ imbalance
extinct	*erloschen*	The Pacific Rim is an area of active and extinct volcanoes.	
	ausgestorben	Dinosaurs are extinct.	≠ existent, living
habitat	*Lebensraum*	the natural home or environment of an animal, plant, or other organism	
harmful	*schädlich*	causing or likely to cause damage	= damaging, dangerous, unsafe
hostile	*feindlich*	Many species survive in a hostile environment.	≠ friendly, pleasant
inedible	*ungenießbar, nicht essbar*	not suitable for eating	= uneatable
nutrient	*Nährstoff*	any substance that animals need to eat and plants need from the soil	
poisonous	*giftig*	Marine life has been badly affected by the poisonous substances that man has been dumping into the oceans.	= toxic
pollutant	*Schadstoff*	a substance which contaminates the atmosphere	
(to) pollute	*verschmutzen*	to make water, air, soil etc. dirty	= to contaminate
polluting	*umweltschädlich*	Less polluting cars will be produced.	
pollution	*Verschmutzung*	In the 1950s and 1960s, nobody thought about pollution.	

Environment

vocabulary	dt. Bedeutung	English phrase	syn/opp
preservation	*Erhaltung*	when you keep sth the same or prevent it from being damaged or destroyed	= conservation
primates	*Primaten*	Primates existed before the dinosaurs became extinct.	
(to) protect	*schützen*	to keep sb or sth safe	= to guard, to safeguard
(to) purify	*reinigen*	Trees help to purify the air.	= to cleanse, to filter ≠ to contaminate
quality of life	*Lebensqualität*	Green spaces in cities improve the quality of life.	
rain forest	*Regenwald*	It is feared that most of the rain forests will have disappeared soon.	
resources	*Ressourcen, Bodenschätze*	coal, oil and wood are natural resources	
(to) restore	*wiederherstellen*	Environmentalists have worked out plans to restore the natural beauty of the area.	
scarcity	*Knappheit, Mangel*	A scientific report named water scarcity as one of the top global risks in the 21st century.	
soil erosion	*Bodenerosion*	The cutting down of the rain forest will increase soil erosion.	
solar system	*Sonnensystem*	The earth is different from all the other planets in our solar system.	

vocabulary	dt. Bedeutung	English phrase	syn/opp
species	*Gattung*	Scientists can tell which species of animal early humans hunted and ate.	
supply	*Vorrat*	Germs are a major health hazard in our food supply.	= stock, resource
surface	*Oberfläche*	Greenhouse gas concentrations are responsible for rising temperatures on the earth's surface.	
survival	*Überleben*	continuing to live or exist	
uninhabitable	*unbewohnbar*	not suited for living in	
vertebrate	*Wirbeltier*	a group of animals (including mammals, birds and fish) with a backbone	
wildlife activist	*Naturschützer*in*	a person who cares for the protection of plants and animals	

2 Air pollution

vocabulary	dt. Bedeutung	English phrase	syn/opp
acid rain	*saurer Regen*	Acid rain causes damage to our forests, buildings and rivers.	
carbon dioxide (CO_2)	*Kohlendioxid (CO_2)*	Worldwide CO_2 emissions must be reduced significantly.	
carbon monoxide (CO)	*Kohlenmonoxid (CO)*	a colourless, odourless, very poisonous gas	
combustion	*Verbrennung*	Fossil fuel combustion is responsible for global warming.	
combustion engine	*Verbrennungsmotor*	Will combustion engines soon be a thing of the past?	

Environment

vocabulary	dt. Bedeutung	English phrase	syn/opp
(to) contaminate	*verseuchen*	Dry cleaners using too many chemicals contaminate our air.	= to pollute
contamination	*Verseuchung*		
depletion	*Verringerung, Schwund, Abbau*	The depletion of the earth's ozone layer is a major concern.	
diesel engine	*Dieselmotor*	Some cities are planning to ban cars with diesel engines.	
electric car	*Elektroauto*	Electric cars are an environmentally friendly alternative to fossil-fuelled cars.	= e-car
emission	*Ausstoß, Emission*	The warming of the earth's atmosphere is the result of the emission of different industrial gases.	
(to) emit	*ausstoßen*		
exhaust fumes	*Auspuffgase, Abgase*	Cleaner engines are developed to reduce toxic exhaust fumes.	
fallout	*(radioaktiver) Niederschlag*	Radioactive fallout killed thousands in Hiroshima and Nagasaki.	
global warming	*Erderwärmung, globale Erwärmung*	People have become more aware of the danger of global warming.	
greenhouse effect	*Treibhauseffekt*	global warming of the atmosphere	
hazard	*Gefahr*	Air pollution is a health hazard.	= risk, danger
hybrid car	*Hybridauto*	Hybrid cars use more than one form of energy (e. g. a combustion engine and an electric motor).	

Environment

vocabulary	dt. Bedeutung	English phrase	syn/opp
hydrocarbon	Kohlenwasserstoff	Car manufacturers are reducing hydrocarbon emissions from motor vehicles.	
(to) load load	belasten Last	We have loaded our air with dangerous chemicals.	= to burden
low-emission	schadstoffarm	London introduced the world's first "Ultra Low Emission Zone".	= green (vehicle)
nitric oxide	Stickoxid	Nitric oxide is a strong pollutant and can cause serious health problems.	
ozone layer	Ozonschicht	Holes in the ozone layer and air pollution are growing sources of concern.	
radiation	Strahlung	Higher levels of ultra-violet radiation cause skin and other cancers.	
respirable dust	Feinstaub	People who are exposed to respirable dust suffer from bronchitis and asthma.	= fine dust
skin cancer	Hautkrebs	Larger amounts of ultra-violet light may induce skin cancer.	
substitute	Ersatz(-stoff)	Scientists are trying to find a substitute for the dangerous CFCs (FCKW).	= replacement, alternative
sulphur dioxide	Schwefeldioxid	a poisonous gas that causes air pollution	
ultraviolet rays	UV-Strahlen	Ultraviolet rays can cause skin cancer.	

3 Water pollution

vocabulary	dt. Bedeutung	English phrase	syn/opp
ailing	*kränkelnd, dahinsiechend*	We must do something to help our ailing oceans.	
detergent	*Reinigungsmittel*	Detergents pollute our rivers.	
(to) discharge	*(Abwasser) einleiten, ablassen*	Too much waste water is discharged into our rivers.	
(to) irrigate	*bewässern*	to provide water for an area of land so that crops can be grown	
microplastics	*Mikroplastik*	Microplastics are small particles of plastics contained in cosmetics, for example.	
plastic pollution	*Verschmutzung durch Plastik*	Plastic pollution is a growing problem – soon there will be more plastic than fish in our oceans.	
sewage	*Abwasser*	waste water from households	
sewage plant	*Kläranlage*	a place where waste water is cleaned	
threat	*Bedrohung*	More attention is being paid to another threat to the seas of the world: algae bloom.	= menace, hazard, risk
(to) threaten	*(be-)drohen*	The coastal areas were threatened by flooding.	= to menace ≠ to protect
waste water	*Abwasser*	used water from households or factories	

4 Waste

vocabulary	dt. Bedeutung	English phrase	syn/opp
biodegradable	biologisch abbaubar	consisting of substances which decompose naturally	
disposable bottle	Einwegflasche	a bottle which is not returned to the shop but thrown away	
disposal	Beseitigung	Special containers are needed for the disposal of harmful rubbish.	
dump	Müllhalde	An open dump attracts rats and other pests.	
dumping ground	Müllhalde, -kippe	Some nations use the oceans as dumping ground for chemical waste.	
garbage	Müll, Abfall	things that we throw away	
junk	Müll, Abfall	old things of little value	= trash, litter, refuse
litter	Müll, Abfall	pieces of paper and other waste	
nuclear waste	Atommüll	The problem concerning the permanent safe disposal of nuclear waste is still unsolved.	
packaging	Verpackung	Unnecessary packaging can be left in the shops.	
(to) recycle	wiederverwerten	to use materials like paper, glass or plastic again	
recycling	Wiederverwertung	Household waste is sorted in special recycling plants.	
return bottle	Mehrwegflasche	a bottle which you return to the shop so that it can be used again	≠ disposable bottle

vocabulary	dt. Bedeutung	English phrase	syn/opp
throw-away	Wegwerf-	We must overcome our throw-away mentality.	
toxic waste	Giftmüll	Where shall we put our toxic waste?	
waste (to) waste	Abfall vergeuden	Local district councils are responsible for waste collection.	
waste collection	Müllabfuhr	City councils spend a lot of money on waste collection.	= refuse/ rubbish collection
waste disposal	Müllbeseitigung, Abfallentsorgung	We need safer methods of waste disposal.	
waste management	Abfallwirtschaft	organising the disposal of waste	
waste minimisation	Müllvermeidung, Müllreduzierung	The best ways to achieve waste minimisation are to reduce packaging and educate consumers about how to throw away less.	
waste separation	Mülltrennung	The local council offers a leaflet on waste separation.	

5 Energy

vocabulary	dt. Bedeutung	English phrase	syn/opp
biofuel	Biokraftstoff	Crops such as sugar cane and palm oil are the basis of biofuel production.	= renewable/ biomass fuel
conservation (to) conserve	Erhaltung, Bewahrung; Einsparung erhalten	Little attention has been paid to the conservation of energy.	= preservation, protection

vocabulary	dt. Bedeutung	English phrase	syn/opp
energy consumption	Energieverbrauch	The developed countries are to reduce energy consumption further.	
energy efficiency	Energieeffizienz, Energieausnutzung	The government introduced measures to improve the energy efficiency of buildings.	
energy transition	Energiewende	An energy transition from nuclear to alternative sources is connected with high costs.	
fossil fuel	fossiler Brennstoff (z. B. Öl, Kohle)	Cleaner car engines have been developed to curb the burning of fossil fuels.	
fracking	Fracking	Fracking is a technology to recover gas from under the earth.	
green energy	umweltfreundliche Energie	Water, wind and solar power are sources of green energy.	= alternative energy
natural gas	Erdgas	Natural gas is used for heating houses.	
nuclear power plant	Atomkraftwerk	In 1986 a Soviet nuclear power plant at Chernobyl exploded.	
power station	Kraftwerk	a place where electricity is generated	
renewable	erneuerbar	Wind power is a renewable source of energy.	
reprocessing plant	Wiederaufbereitungsanlage	Demonstrators blocked the entry to the reprocessing plant at Sellafield.	

Science and technology

1 Genetic engineering

vocabulary	dt. Bedeutung	English phrase	syn/opp
(to) abort abortion	ein Baby/einen Fötus abtreiben Abtreibung	to end a pregnancy that is not wanted	
(to) abort	etw. abbrechen	Due to engine failure the space mission was aborted.	= to cancel, to call off
ailing	krank, kränkelnd, notleidend	giving physical or emotional pain or trouble	= unwell, weak ≠ vigorous
(to) alter	(ver-)ändern	Genetic engineers alter the inherited characteristics of an organism.	= to change, to modify
application	Anwendung	Scientific research and its technological application should be subordinated to moral and spiritual values.	
bacteria [Sg. bacterium]	Bakterien	large group of unicellular micro-organisms	
beneficial	nützlich	Knowledge of nutrition is beneficial to the health of people.	= advantageous, helpful ≠ harmful, detrimental
benefit	Nutzen	Opinions are divided over the potential hazards or benefits of genetic engineering.	
biotechnology	Biotechnologie	making use of biological processes for industrial and other purposes	
birth defect	Geburtsfehler	a physical or biochemical weakness a person is born with	

Science and technology

vocabulary	dt. Bedeutung	English phrase	syn/opp
by chance	zufällig	not intended, unintentionally	≠ intentional
characteristic	Kennzeichen, Merkmal	The main characteristic of this plant is that it resists disease.	= feature
cloning	Klonen	production of genetically identical individuals by transplanting whole cell nuclei	
(to) conduct	durchführen	Dangerous experiments can only be conducted under strict safety conditions.	= to carry out
(to) contract a disease	eine Krankheit bekommen, erkranken	to develop or catch an illness	
(to) convert	verwandeln	to change from one form or function to another	
cure	Heilung	Genetic engineering offers hope of cures for inherited diseases.	= remedy, medication
(to) decipher	entschlüsseln, entziffern	to succeed in understanding sth such as a code, an old document etc.	= to decode ≠ to encode
desirable	erstrebenswert, begehrenswert	wanted or wished for	
destiny	Schicksal	sb's predetermined future	= fate
(to) determine	bestimmen, festlegen	RNA and DNA, the proteins in every cell, determine the basic inherited characteristics of life.	
disease	Krankheit	Genetic engineering offers hope of cures for inherited diseases.	= illness

Science and technology

vocabulary	dt. Bedeutung	English phrase	syn/opp
DNA (deoxyribonucleic acid)	DNS (Desoxyribonukleinsäure)	In 1953, James Watson and Francis Crick demonstrated that genetic material is composed of two nucleic acids, DNA and RNA.	
(to) donate donor	spenden Spender*in	People should donate more blood and organs for transplantation.	
embryo	Embryo, ungeborenes menschliches Wesen	In 1997 scientists duplicated a human embryo, provoking cries that technology had gone too far.	
embryology	Embryologie	the scientific study of the formation and development of embryos	
(to) enhance	verbessern	Many spices as well as natural and synthetic flavours enhance the taste of foods.	= to improve
(to) eradicate	ausrotten	to destroy completely	= to extinguish, to exterminate
ethical	ethisch, sittlich, moralisch	relating to morals, the science of ethics or standards of conduct	
evolution	Evolution, Entwicklung	The present state of all forms of life, from bacteria to humans, has been achieved by evolution.	
fertile	fruchtbar	plants: able to bear fruit; humans: able to conceive a child	≠ infertile, barren
fertilisation	Befruchtung	the act or process of impregnating	

Science and technology

vocabulary	dt. Bedeutung	English phrase	syn/opp
(to) fertilise	befruchten	Scientists have found ways to fertilise human eggs outside the body.	
food additive	Lebensmittel-zusatz(-stoff)	Dozens of food additives ought to be prohibited as health risks.	
gene	Gen	a part of a cell that is passed on from a parent to a child and that controls particular characteristics	
gene technology	Gentechnologie	We hope that gene technology will help to treat many inherited diseases.	
genetic code	genetischer Code	The complete human genetic code has been deciphered.	
genetic engineering	Gentechnik	using technology to change the genes in the cells of plants or animals	
genetically modified food (GM food)	gentechnisch veränderte Nahrungsmittel	People have genuine concerns about genetically modified (GM) food.	
geneticist	Genforscher*in, Genetiker*in	a scientist who has specialised in genetic engineering	
genome	Genom	the full complement of genetic information that an individual organism inherits from its parents	
genuine	echt	Due to medical progress curing hereditary diseases has become a genuine possibility.	= real, true

vocabulary	dt. Bedeutung	English phrase	syn/opp
haemophilia	*Bluterkrankheit*	It may be possible to cure hereditary diseases, such as haemophilia, using gene technology.	
hazard	*Gefahr*	Opinions are divided over the potential hazards or benefits of genetic engineering.	= risk, danger
heredity	*Vererbung*	the passing on of genetic factors, such as the colour of hair or eyes, from one generation to the next	
human	*menschlich*	Scientists in the USA have experimented with dividing a human embryo.	
hybrid	*Kreuzung, Mischform*	an offspring (*Nachkomme*) of two animals or plants of different races or breeds	
identical	*identisch, eineiig (Zwillinge)*	Identical twins are exact copies of one another and develop from the same egg.	
immune	*immun*	protected against and resistant to infection	
impact	*Auswirkung, Einfluss*	Medical progress will have a deep impact on our society.	= effect, consequence
(to) implant	*einsetzen, einpflanzen, implantieren*	Doctors help women have babies by mixing sperm and eggs in a test tube and then implanting the embryos in the womb (*Mutterleib*).	
implication	*Auswirkung, Folge*	The implications of genetic engineering are not clear to us.	

vocabulary	dt. Bedeutung	English phrase	syn/opp
incurable	unheilbar	Diseases considered incurable today might be eradicated in the long run.	
infertile	unfruchtbar	There are several treatments open to doctors to try and help infertile couples.	
(to) inherit inheritance	erben Erbe	Genetic engineers alter the inherited characteristics of an organism.	
inherited disease	Erbkrankheit	Genetic engineering offers hope of cures for inherited diseases.	= hereditary disease
insemination	Befruchtung	The method of artificial insemination is used to help childless couples.	
(to) insert	einsetzen, einfügen	Genetic material from one species of plant or animal is inserted into another species.	
(to) isolate	isolieren	Scientists can isolate sections of DNA which represent single genes.	
IVF (in vitro fertilisation)	künstliche Befruchtung (wörtlich: Befruchtung im Reagenzglas)	In 1978 IVF was first successfully applied to human reproduction.	= artificial insemination
laboratory	Labor	a room or building for scientific experiments	
longevity	Langlebigkeit	long life, living for a long time	

Science and technology

vocabulary	dt. Bedeutung	English phrase	syn/opp
mammal	*Säugetier*	The first success in cloning an adult mammal was achieved by a team of British researchers in 1996.	
(to) manage	*(etw.) fertig bringen, schaffen*	Scientists managed to divide a human embryo in the early stages of fertilisation.	
(to) manipulate	*manipulieren, verändern*	Genetic engineering modifies the characteristics of an organism by manipulating its genetic material.	
metabolism	*Stoffwechsel*	all the chemical processes in the body, esp. those that cause food to be used for energy and growth	
(to) modify	*(ver-)ändern*	Genes can be modified with chemicals or radiation.	= to change, to alter
mutation	*Mutation, Veränderung*	the change in genetic material, e. g. caused by radiation	= alteration, modification
natural selection	*natürliche Auswahl*	Natural selection favours or suppresses a particular gene.	
(to) originate	*entstehen, seinen Anfang nehmen*	Life on earth originated more than 3.4 billion years ago.	= to begin, to start
potential	*möglich*	We have yet to discover the potential risks of genetic engineering.	= possible
pregnant pregnancy	*schwanger Schwangerschaft*	Women who have trouble becoming pregnant can turn to methods of artificial insemination.	= expectant, expecting

vocabulary	dt. Bedeutung	English phrase	syn/opp
prenatal	vorgeburtlich	before birth, during pregnancy	
preventive treatment	(Gesundheits-)Vorsorge, Vorsorgemaßnahme	Preventive treatment can help avoid chronic diseases.	
progeny	Nachkommen	offspring, children	
promising	(viel-)versprechend	New promising strategies have been developed to help people with a genetic deficiency.	= encouraging
property	Eigenschaft	A gene can be reproduced with a medically desirable property.	= characteristic, feature
(to) provoke	hervorrufen, auslösen	The experiment with a human embryo provoked great alarm.	= to raise, to stir
(to) refine refinement	verbessern Verbesserung, Verfeinerung	Scientists have succeeded in refining the technique of cloning.	= to improve
reluctant	widerwillig, widerstrebend	unwilling to do sth	= loath, hesitant
(to) represent	für etw. stehen	Scientists can isolate sections of DNA which represent single genes.	
(to) reproduce	reproduzieren, nachbilden, (sich) fortpflanzen	Genes can be reproduced in the laboratory.	= to generate, to duplicate
research researcher	Forschung Forscher*in	scientific investigation and study	
(to) resemble	ähneln	The earliest existing organisms were cells, resembling modern bacteria.	= to look like

Science and technology

vocabulary	dt. Bedeutung	English phrase	syn/opp
resistant	*widerstandsfähig, immun*	Critics of biotechnology say it could lead to resistant weeds and insects.	
species	*Art, Spezies, Gattung*	Darwin's book *On the Origin of Species by Means of Natural Selection* was published in 1859.	
stem cell	*Stammzelle*	Stem cell research may lead to new treatments for diabetes, Alzheimer's, heart disease and cancer.	
strict	*streng*	Dangerous experiments can only be conducted under strict conditions of containment *(Abschottung)*.	= rigid
test-tube baby	*Retortenbaby*	Louise Brown, born 25 July, 1978, was the first test-tube baby.	
(to) tinker	*herumpfuschen*	Will people wish to eat foods they know have been tinkered with by scientists?	= to mess around, to play around
tissue	*Gewebe*	the material that animals and plants are made of	
topic	*Thema*	Human clones are no longer a topic for science fiction.	= subject, subject matter
(to) transfer	*übertragen*	to move sb or sth from one place to another	
(to) transform	*verwandeln*	Scientific progress will transform the world we live in.	= to change, to alter

Science and technology

vocabulary	dt. Bedeutung	English phrase	syn/opp
transplant	*Verpflanzung, Transplantation*	The South African surgeon Christiaan Barnard performed the first human heart transplant in 1967.	
(to) transplant	*verpflanzen*		
treatment	*Behandlung*	After treatment in the fertility clinic Mrs Denton had triplets.	
(to) trigger	*auslösen*	Scientists are trying to find the mechanisms that trigger certain diseases.	
triplet	*Drilling*	one of three children born at one birth	
variety	*Sorte*	A biotech firm in California has developed a tomato that does not rot as fast as normal varieties.	= sort, kind
virus	*Virus*	Government research centres are trying to decode the DNA in dangerous viruses.	

2 Computers and digital technology

vocabulary	dt. Bedeutung	English phrase	syn/opp
access	*Zugang*	Some activists demand free access to the Internet.	
account	*Benutzerkonto*	Even the Pope has an account on Facebook.	
AI (artificial intelligence)	*KI (künstliche Intelligenz)*	Firms are using AI to forecast demand, hire workers and deal with customers.	
app (short for: application)	*Anwendung, Programm, App*	Computer specialists earn good money developing apps for mobile devices.	

Science and technology

vocabulary	dt. Bedeutung	English phrase	syn/opp
A.R. (augmented reality)	Augmented Reality, erweiterte Realität	Augmented reality apps impose digital content on real-world surroundings.	
automation	Automatisierung	Automation means that more and more tasks are performed by machines and robots.	
cloud	Cloud (wörtlich: Wolke)	an image used for the Internet; many users store their data in the cloud	
compatible	vereinbar, kompatibel	When you buy a new programme, make sure it is compatible with your computer's operating system (Betriebssystem).	
(to be) computer literate	Computerkenntnisse besitzen(d)	to be able to use computers well	
cyber	Cyber-	a prefix that is used to relate sth to the Internet, e. g. -war, -crime, -law	
cybercrime	Internetkriminalität	Cyberstalking is an example of cybercrime.	
database	Datenspeicher, Datenbank	Every programme on your computer keeps its own database.	
data processing	Datenverarbeitung	Data processing is carried out by computers.	
device	Gerät	The number of electronic devices people use today has increased enormously.	
digital immigrant	Digital Immigrant	Digital immigrants have had to learn how to use digital technology later in life.	≠ digital native

Science and technology

vocabulary	dt. Bedeutung	English phrase	syn/opp
digital native	Digital Native	Digital natives have grown up with digital technology.	≠ digital immigrant
digitisation	Digitalisierung	Digitisation and automation have revolutionised the way we live and work.	
feature	Funktion	Word processors offer more features than most users need every day.	
file	Datei	Think about how to organise your files properly on your hard disk.	
(USB) flash drive	Speicherstick	a small stick for storing digital data; it can be connected to a computer through a serial port	= USB stick
folder	Ordner	Save your computer files in different folders on your disk, just like in a box.	
(to) key in	Daten in einen Computer eingeben	to enter data with a computer keyboard	
malware (short for: malicious software)	Schadprogramm	a software with harmful effects, such as changing or deleting files	
memory	Speicher	the capacity of a computer for storing data	
outdated	veraltet	Whatever we learn is outdated before we can apply it.	= antiquated, obsolete ≠ up-to-date
(to) paste	einfügen	to copy or move text into a document from another text passage or document	
(to) process	verarbeiten, bearbeiten	to operate on data by means of a computer programme	

vocabulary	dt. Bedeutung	English phrase	syn/opp
release	*Ausgabe*	Make sure to use the latest release of the anti-virus scanner.	
(to) retrieve	*Informationen abrufen*	to find or extract information stored in a computer	
(to) scan	*durchsuchen*	Use an anti-virus programme to scan your hard disk for malware.	
self-driving car	*selbstfahrendes Auto*	Do you think that self-driving cars will cause fewer accidents than human drivers?	= autonomous car, self-driving vehicle
smart	*intelligent*	Smart devices (such as smartphones or smart TVs) can connect with other devices and the Internet.	
spreadsheet	*Tabellenkalkulation(sprogramm)*	Microsoft's "Excel" is a widely used spreadsheet.	
(to) store	*speichern*	You can store data in the cloud.	
(to) swipe	*wischen*	On a tablet you swipe with one finger to change pages.	
virus	*Virus*	a software which can reproduce itself and cause great harm to files or other programmes	
V.R. (virtual reality)	*VR (virtuelle Realität)*	Virtual reality headsets make it possible to immerse oneself in a computer-generated environment.	
wireless	*drahtlos*	Most hotels offer wireless Internet connection.	

Media

1 Television, radio and streaming services

vocabulary	dt. Bedeutung	English phrase	syn/opp
binge watching **(to) binge-watch**	*Binge-Watching bingen (sehr viele Folgen einer Serie innerhalb kurzer Zeit ansehen)*	Online streaming services induce more and more people to engage in binge watching.	
(to) broadcast	*senden*	Episode 245 of our series will be broadcast next Monday at 9.30 p.m.	= to transmit
channel	*(Fernseh-)Kanal, Programm*	If you don't like this programme, switch over to another channel.	
coverage	*Berichterstattung*	CNN is well-known for its live coverage of world events.	
documentary	*Dokumentarfilm*	a film that gives information on a particular subject	
feature	*Spielfilm*	a full-length film, the main film	
feature	*Reportage*	After the news we'll bring you a special feature on drug abuse among young school leavers.	
feedback	*Rückmeldung*	The more feedback we get from viewers, the better.	
interference	*(Empfangs-)Störung*	When you listen to the 'Deutsche Welle' in South America, you get a lot of interference from foreign broadcasting stations.	

vocabulary	dt. Bedeutung	English phrase	syn/opp
network	Netz, Netzwerk	The bank uses a computer network to transfer data to all its branches in the country.	
piracy	Raubkopieren	Piracy is a big concern of the digital publishing industry, because digital media can be copied easily.	
ratings	(Einschalt-)Quoten, Zuschauerzahlen	Ratings decide whether the series will be continued or not.	
remote control	Fernbedienung	With a remote control you can turn on your TV set from where you are sitting.	
satellite	Satellit	The new television satellite sends a very strong signal to earth.	
satellite dish	Satellitenschüssel	an aerial (Antenne) in the shape of a bowl	
satellite TV	Satellitenfernsehen	Do you prefer satellite TV, cable or online streaming?	
screen	Bildschirm	Many people maintain that there is too much sex and violence on the screen.	
screenplay	Drehbuch	the script of a film	
soap opera	Seifenoper	*Coronation Street* is the longest running British TV soap opera.	
sponsor	Sponsor*in, Förderer/Förderin	a person or an organisation that provides the money for a programme or an activity	

Media

vocabulary	dt. Bedeutung	English phrase	syn/opp
streaming	Streaming (kontinuierliche Übertragung von Audio- und Videodaten)	With online streaming services you can watch videos and listen to music directly, without having to download them first.	
subtitle	Untertitel	I saw a Spanish film with English subtitles.	
(to) tune in	(ein Programm) einstellen/einschalten, zuhören	And don't forget to tune in at 8 o'clock tomorrow when we'll present the 'WORLD 100' best-selling singles of all time.	
(to) turn down	(Lautstärke) leiser stellen	Please turn down that terrible noise!	
(to) turn off	(Radio, TV) ausschalten	I tried to watch an episode of the new TV series, but after 10 minutes I just had to turn off the set.	= to switch off ≠ to switch on
(to) turn on	(Radio, Fernseher) an-, einschalten	With a remote control you can turn on your TV set from where you are sitting.	= to switch on ≠ to switch off
viewer	(Fernseh-) Zuschauer*in	I'm sure the TV viewer doesn't want more and more commercials to interrupt the programmes.	
volume	Lautstärke	The volume can be controlled by pressing this button.	
(to) watch TV	fernsehen	How many hours a day do you watch TV?	

2 Newspapers, magazines and (e-)books

vocabulary	dt. Bedeutung	English phrase	syn/opp
advice column	Ratgeberrubrik, -spalte (in Zeitschriften)	In an advice column, an expert (the "agony aunt") gives advice on problems the readers send in.	
appendix	Anhang (eines Buches)	A list of hotels is given in the appendix of our tourist guide book.	
breaking news	Eilmeldung	Our website brings you the latest breaking news.	
brochure	Broschüre	a small book or magazine containing pictures and information	= leaflet, pamphlet
censorship	Zensur	Especially in times of war there is a strict military censorship on media reports.	
circulation	(Zeitungs-)Auflage	The newspaper's daily circulation has decreased over the last years.	
column	(Zeitungs-)Spalte	a vertical arrangement of a page or text	
copy	Exemplar (eines Buches oder einer Zeitung)	I kept a copy of our daily paper with the reports on the German reunification.	
copyright	Urheberrecht	Who holds the copyright of the song?	
cover	(Buch-)Einband	On the front cover was a picture of a woman in red.	
daily	Tageszeitung	Many Britons read more than one daily.	≠ weekly, monthly
e-book	E-Book	book available in electronic form	

Media

vocabulary	dt. Bedeutung	English phrase	syn/opp
edition	(Buch-)Ausgabe	This is a valuable first edition of Robert Burns' poems.	
editor	Redakteur*in	a journalist who is responsible for the final version of a text	
electronic publishing	elektronisches Publizieren	written information published not on paper but on DVDs, CD-ROMs or online	= digital publishing
encyclopaedia	(sehr umfangreiches) Lexikon	Wikipedia is a free online encyclopaedia.	
e-reader	Lesegerät für E-Books	Several multinational corporations compete on the market for e-readers.	
extract	Auszug	I hope you'll remember the extract from the US Declaration of Independence which you learnt.	= excerpt
freedom of expression	Meinungsfreiheit	Freedom of expression has always been a characteristic of a free and liberal society.	
freedom of the press	Pressefreiheit	All democratic states guarantee the freedom of the press.	
front page	Titelseite	the first page of a newspaper	
heading	Überschrift	Try to find a new heading for this paragraph.	= headline
headline	Schlagzeile	the title of a newspaper story	
index	Register	an alphabetical list printed at the back of a book	

Media

vocabulary	dt. Bedeutung	English phrase	syn/opp
issue	(Zeitungs-)Ausgabe, Nummer	In our next issue we'll publish a full report on the latest computer video games.	
leaflet	Prospekt, Flugblatt	The bank produced a little leaflet on 'How to open an account with us'.	
letter to the editor	Leserbrief	I've never written a letter to the editor in my life.	
manual	Handbuch	Why don't you read the instruction manual before you unpack the stereo set?	
mass media	Massenmedien	Mass media reach a large number of people.	
media	Medien	the main means of mass communication, e. g. the Internet, newspapers, radio and television	
message	Nachricht, Mitteilung, Botschaft	a communication in writing, in speech, or by signals	
national paper	überregionale Zeitung	*The Times* is the most famous British national paper.	≠ regional or local paper
news	Nachricht(en)	He heard the bad news on the radio.	
newsagent	Zeitungsladen, -händler*in	a shop which sells papers, magazines, sweets and stationery	= paper shop
newsstand	Zeitungskiosk	an outdoor place where newspapers are sold	
novel	Roman	Stephen King published his first novel *Carrie* in 1973.	

vocabulary	dt. Bedeutung	English phrase	syn/opp
online newspaper	Onlinezeitung	A lot of people prefer online newspapers to printed ones.	
outline	Übersicht, Umriss, Gliederung	I'm going to give you a brief outline of the plot of the book *Gone with the Wind*.	
paperback	Taschenbuch	a book with a flexible paper binding	
paragraph	(Text-)Absatz	a subdivision of an article or essay	
pay wall	Paywall, Bezahlschranke	Many online newspapers have a pay wall so that their content can only be accessed by paid subscribers.	
periodical	Zeitschrift	a serious – often academic – magazine, e. g. *The Economist*	
plot	Handlung, Fabel (eines Romans)	the main story	
(to) publish	veröffentlichen, herausgeben	to prepare and issue a book or piece of music	
publisher	Verlag, Verleger*in	For years I've been trying to find a publisher for my novel *In Sadness We Unite*.	
push notification	Push-Benachrichtigung	My favourite newspaper sends me push notifications whenever there is new content online.	
quality paper	seriöse Tageszeitung	*The Daily Telegraph* is a highly respected quality paper.	≠ tabloid, redtop
quotation	Zitat	Every morning our teacher used to greet us with a quotation from Shakespeare.	

vocabulary	dt. Bedeutung	English phrase	syn/opp
(to) quote	zitieren	to repeat the exact words somebody said or wrote	
readership	Leserschaft	*The Sun* and *The Daily Telegraph* cater for a different readership.	
(to) report report	berichten Bericht	The newspapers report every single step of the Royal Family.	
review	Rezension, Kritik	a critical evaluation of a book or play	
source	(Informations-) Quelle	I've obtained this confidential information from a very reliable source.	
(to) squeeze	herauspressen, herausquetschen	The press people tried to squeeze more information from the speaker of the president.	= to obtain
subscriber	Abonnent*in	A subscriber of the test magazine *Which* gets valuable information about the quality of a wide range of products.	
(to) suspect	argwöhnen, vermuten	Many readers suspect the glossy photos of models in magazines have been digitally enhanced.	
tabloid	Boulevardzeitung, Klatschzeitung	a newspaper with small pages, short news stories and a lot of photographs	
volume	(Buch-)Band	a book which is part of a work or series	
yellow press	Sensationspresse	another name for the tabloids	

3 Social media

vocabulary	dt. Bedeutung	English phrase	syn/opp
algorithm	*Algorithmus*	Algorithms determine the kind of news, ads etc. we get to see online.	
channel	*Kanal*	Please subscribe to my YouTube channel.	
(to) collect data	*Daten sammeln*	Companies like Google, Amazon or Facebook collect huge amounts of data about their users.	
crowdfunding	*Crowdfunding*	The band used crowdfunding to finance their latest album.	
cyberbullying	*Cybermobbing*	Cyberbullying on social networks is a serious problem.	
data privacy	*Datenschutz*	Experts warn that Internet giants and social networks infringe data privacy laws.	= data security
emoji	*Emoji*	My friends' WhatsApp messages are full of emojis.	
fake news	*Falschmeldung(en)*	Not every source on the Internet is trustworthy – some sites also spread fake news.	
filter bubble	*Filterblase*	Users of social media are said to live in a filter bubble – they only get to see content that supports their world view.	
follower (to) follow	*Follower folgen*	Celebrities often have millions of followers on Facebook, Twitter or Instagram.	

vocabulary	dt. Bedeutung	English phrase	syn/opp
(to) go viral	viral werden, sich schnell verbreiten	The cute cat video has gone viral overnight.	= to spread quickly
hashtag	Hashtag	Hashtags are used to categorise information on Twitter.	
influencer	Influencer*in	Influencers often use their popularity on social media to advertise products.	
(to) leave a trail	Spuren hinterlassen	When surfing the net, we usually leave a digital trail.	
(to) post post	posten (Social Media-)Post	My sister always posts food photos on Facebook.	
profile	Profil	Employers often check their applicants' profiles on social networks.	
(to) share	teilen	I never share private information online.	
social media	soziale Medien	Some of the most well-known social media sites include Twitter, Facebook and Instagram.	
social network	soziales Netzwerk	Social networks connect people from all over the world.	= social networking site
(to) tag tag	markieren, taggen Tag, Etikett, Beschriftung	My brother tags all the photos he posts on Facebook.	
(to be) trending	angesagt (sein)	What's trending today?	
vlog vlogger	Vlog Vlogger*in	combination of the words "video" and "blog"	

Britisches und amerikanisches Englisch

deutsche Bedeutung	British English [BE]	American English [AE]
1. Stock	first floor	second floor
Abfall	rubbish	garbage
Apotheke	chemist's	pharmacy, drugstore
Aufzug	lift	elevator
Autobahn	motorway	highway, freeway
Babywindel	nappy	diaper
Bahn	railway	railroad
Benzin	petrol	gas, gasoline
Bonbon	sweet	candy
Briefkasten	post-box	mailbox
Brieftasche	wallet	billfold
Bürgersteig	pavement	sidewalk
Chips	crisps [Pl.]	potato chips [Pl.]
City, Innenstadt	city centre	downtown
ein Auto mieten	(to) hire a car	(to) rent a car
Eis am Stiel	ice lolly	popsicle
Entschuldigung	sorry	excuse me
Erdgeschoss	ground floor	first floor
Fahrplan	timetable	schedule
Führerschein	driving licence	driver's license
Fußball	football	soccer
Fußgängerunterführung	subway	(pedestrian) underpass
Garderobe	cloakroom	checkroom
Gaspedal	accelerator	gas pedal
Geldschein	note	bill
Geschäft	shop	store

deutsche Bedeutung	British English [BE]	American English [AE]
Gleis(e)	rails [Pl.]	tracks [Pl.]
Handtasche	handbag	purse, pocketbook
Herbst	autumn	fall
Hose	trousers [Pl.]	pants [Pl.]
Hosenträger [Pl.]	braces [Pl.]	suspenders [Pl.]
Keks	biscuit	cookie
Kinderwagen	pram	baby carriage
Kino	cinema	movie theater
(Kino-)Film	film	movie
Kofferraum	boot	trunk
Kreisverkehr	roundabout	traffic circle
Limousine	saloon	sedan
Marmelade	jam	jelly
Motorhaube	bonnet	hood
natürlich	of course	sure
öffentliche Verkehrsmittel	public transport	public transportation
Päckchen, Paket	parcel	package
Pommes frites	chips [Pl.]	(French) fries [Pl.]
Portemonnaie	purse	wallet, coin purse
Postleitzahl	postcode	zip code
Privatschule	public school	private school
Punkt	full stop	period, bei Internetadressen: dot
Radiergummi	rubber	eraser
Rechnung	bill	check
Reißverschluss	zip	zipper
schicken	send	mail
Schrank	cupboard	closet

deutsche Bedeutung	British English [BE]	American English [AE]
Schulferien, Weihnachtsferien	holidays [Pl.]	vacation
Talkshow	chat show	talk show
Tankstelle	petrol station	gas station
Taschenlampe	torch	flashlight
Taxi	taxi	cab
U-Bahn	underground	subway
Unterhemd	vest	undershirt
Urlaub	holiday	vacation
Warteschlange	queue	line
Watte	cotton wool	cotton
WC	toilet	bathroom, restroom
Weste	waistcoat	vest
Wie bitte?	pardon?, sorry?	excuse me?
Windschutzscheibe	windscreen	windshield
Wohnung	flat	apartment

False Friends

„falscher Freund"	engl. Bedeutung	false friend	dt. Bedeutung
absolvieren	(to) complete sth	(to) absolve	*lossprechen*
Advokat	lawyer, solicitor	advocate	*Verfechter*in, Befürworter*in*
Aktion	sale, operation, advertising campaign	action	*Tat, Handlung*
aktuell	topical, current	actual	*eigentlich, wirklich*
alle Tage	every day	all day	*den ganzen Tag*
Allee	avenue, tree-lined walk	alley	*Gasse, Durchgang*
also	so, therefore	also	*auch, außerdem*
Ambulanz	outpatients' department	ambulance	*Krankenwagen*
apart	charming, unusual	apart	*auseinander, abseits*
Argument	point	argument	*Wortwechsel, Streit*
Art	kind, sort, type	art	*(bildende) Kunst*
Artist	(circus) performer, artiste	artist	*Künstler*in*
ausgesprochen	pronounced, distinct	outspoken	*offen, aufrichtig*
bald	soon	bald	*glatzköpfig, kahl*
bekommen	(to) receive, (to) get	(to) become	*werden*
Billion	trillion	billion	*Milliarde*
Box	loudspeaker	box	*Kasten*
brav	well-behaved, good	brave	*tapfer, unerschrocken*
Brief	letter	brief (to) brief sb briefs	*kurz, knapp* *jdn. (kurz) informieren* *Slip, Unterhose*
Catcher	wrestler	catcher	*Fänger*in*
Chef	boss	chef	*(Chef-)Koch/Köchin*

„falscher Freund"	engl. Bedeutung	false friend	dt. Bedeutung
City	downtown, city centre	city	Stadt
delikat	delicious; sensitive	delicate	empfindlich, zerbrechlich
dezent	discreet	decent	anständig, ordentlich
Direktion	management	direction	Richtung
Distanz	reserve, coldness	distance	Entfernung
Dom	cathedral	dome	Kuppel(-dach)
Dose	box, can, tin	dose	Dosis
Etikett	label, price tag	etiquette	Etikette, Umgangsformen
eventuell	possible	eventual	endlich, schließlich
extravagant	sophisticated	extravagant	übertrieben
Fabrik	factory	fabric	Stoff, Gewebe
fade	bland, tasteless, colourless, boring	(to) fade	ausbleichen, verblassen
familiär	family-related	familiar	vertraut
Fantasie	imagination	fantasy	Vorstellung, Tagtraum
fast	nearly, almost	fast	schnell
fatal	annoying, awkward	fatal	tödlich, verhängnisvoll
Fleisch	meat	flesh	Muskelfleisch (beim Menschen)
Formular	form	formula	Formel
Fotograf	photographer	photograph	Fotografie
Fraktion	political party/ parliamentary group	fraction	Bruchzahl, Bruchteil
Garage	garage (of a house)	garage	Tankstelle, Autowerkstatt
genial	ingenious, brilliant	genial	witzig, freundlich
Gift	poison	gift	Geschenk

False Friends

„falscher Freund"	engl. Bedeutung	false friend	dt. Bedeutung
Gymnasium	~ grammar school [BE], high school [AE]	gym	*Turnhalle*
Handy	cellular phone, mobile	handy	*praktisch, nützlich*
Herd	stove, cooker	herd	*Herde*
hissen	(to) hoist/fly a flag	(to) hiss	*zischen*
Hochschule	college, university	high school	*Gymnasium, Oberschule*
Kanne	pot, kettle	can	*Dose*
Kantine	cafeteria, canteen	canteen	*Besteckkasten, Feldflasche*
Kaution	bail, deposit	caution	*Vorsicht*
Klosett	toilet, privy	closet	*Wandschrank, Verschlag*
komfortabel	luxurious	comfortable	*behaglich, bequem*
komisch	strange	comic(al)	*lustig*
Konkurrenz	competition, competitor	concurrence	*Übereinstimmung*
konsequent	consistent	consequently	*infolgedessen, folglich*
Kritik	criticism	critic	*Kritiker*in*
Mappe	folder, file, brief-case	map	*Landkarte*
Marmelade	jam	marmalade	*Orangenmarmelade*
Meinung	opinion	meaning	*Bedeutung, Sinn*
Menü	set meal/lunch/dinner, daily special	menu	*Speisekarte*
Mist	dung	mist	*Nebel*
Mörder	murderer	murder	*Mord*
Oldtimer	vintage car, veteran car	old timer	*alter Hase, Veteran*
ordinär	vulgar	ordinary	*alltäglich, gewöhnlich*
Pension	boarding house, guesthouse	pension	*Rente*

„falscher Freund"	engl. Bedeutung	false friend	dt. Bedeutung
plump	clumsy, awkward	plump	mollig, füllig
Präservativ	condom	preservative	Konservierungsmittel
Preis	price	prize	Siegerpreis
primitiv	bare, frugal	primitive	vorzeitlich
prinzipiell	on principle	principally	hauptsächlich
Promotion	doctorate, graduation	promotion	Beförderung
Prospekt	folder, prospectus	prospect	Aussicht
Provision	commission	provision	Versorgung, Vorsorge
Prozess	law suit, trial	process	Verfahren
raffiniert	clever, cunning, sly	refined	verfeinert, gebildet
Rat	advice	rat	Ratte
Rente	pension	rent	Miete
Rezept	recipe	receipt	Quittung
Roman	novel	Roman	Römer*in
Sekt	sparkling wine	sect	Sekte
sensibel	sensitive	sensible	vernünftig
seriös	reliable, respectable	serious	ernsthaft
sich blamieren	(to) embarrass oneself	(to) blame sb	jdn. beschuldigen
spenden	(to) donate sth	(to) spend	ausgeben
Stadium	stage, level	stadium	Stadion
Star	film star, celebrity	star	Stern
sympathisch	nice, pleasant	sympathetic	verständnisvoll, mitfühlend
Trainer	coach	trainers	Turnschuhe
Unternehmer	business person, entrepreneur	undertaker	Leichenbestatter*in
Warenhaus (Kaufhaus)	department store	warehouse	Lagerhalle

Grundwortschatz

vocabulary	dt. Bedeutung	vocabulary	dt. Bedeutung
(to) abandon	aufgeben, preisgeben, verlassen	adventure	Abenteuer
ability	Fähigkeit	advertisement	Werbung, (Zeitungs-)Anzeige
above	über	advertising	Werbung, Reklame
abroad	ins, im Ausland	advice	Rat(-schlag)
absence	Abwesenheit	(to) affect	sich auswirken auf
abundant	reich, reichlich	(to) afford	sich leisten
(to) accept	annehmen	agreement	Vereinbarung
accident	Unfall	ahead	vorn, in Führung
(to) accompany	begleiten	(to) aim	zielen
(to) accomplish	vollenden, ausführen, (Zweck) erreichen	alive	lebendig (noch am Leben)
according to	gemäß, nach, entsprechend	(to) allow	erlauben
account	Konto	almost	fast, beinahe
(to) account	Rechenschaft ablegen	(to) alter	(sich) ändern, verändern
accustomed to	gewöhnt an	although	obwohl, obgleich
acquaintance	Bekanntschaft	altogether	insgesamt
(to) acquire	erlangen, erreichen	ambition	Ehrgeiz, Streben
(to) act	handeln	amount	Betrag
(to) add	zusammenzählen	amusement	Vergnügen, Unterhaltung
(to) address	ansprechen	anchor	(Schiffs-)Anker
(to) administer	verwalten	ancient	sehr alt
(to) admire	bewundern	anger	Ärger, Wut, Zorn
admission	Eintritt	angle	Winkel; Standpunkt
(to) admit	zugeben	angry	zornig
advantage	Vorteil		

vocabulary	dt. Bedeutung	vocabulary	dt. Bedeutung
(to) announce	ankündigen, bekannt geben	(to) assert	behaupten, geltend machen
(to) annoy	ärgern, belästigen	(to) assist	beistehen, helfen, unterstützen
annual	jährlich, Jahres-		
anxiety	Angst, Besorgnis	(to) assume	glauben, annehmen
anxious	gespannt; besorgt	(to) assure	(jdm. etw.) versichern
apart	getrennt, für sich	astonished	erstaunt
(to) appeal	gefallen; Berufung einlegen, appellieren	at least	wenigstens
		(to) attach	befestigen
(to) appear	erscheinen	(to) attain	(Ziel) erreichen, erlangen
appearance	Erscheinen, Aufkommen		
		attempt	Versuch
application	Bewerbung	(to) attend	anwesend sein
(to) apply for	sich bewerben um	attention	Aufmerksamkeit
(to) appoint	ernennen	attitude	Haltung, Einstellung
(to) approach	sich nähern	(to) attract	anziehen
(to) approve	billigen	audience	Publikum
(to) argue	streiten, einwenden; erörtern, diskutieren	available	erhältlich, verfügbar
		average	Durchschnitt
(to) arise	sich bieten	(to) avoid	vermeiden
(to) arrange	vereinbaren	aware	bewusst
arrangement	Vorkehrung	awe	Ehrfurcht, Scheu, Furcht
(to) arrest	festnehmen, verhaften		
(to) arrive	ankommen	awful	schrecklich
artificial	künstlich, Kunst-	baggage [AE]	Gepäck
(to) ascend	steigen, aufsteigen, emporsteigen	balance	Gleichgewicht
		bank	Bank (Institut); Ufer
ashamed	beschämt	bare	bloß, nackt
(to) ask for	bitten um	barely	kaum
(to) assemble	sich versammeln		

vocabulary	dt. Bedeutung	vocabulary	dt. Bedeutung
(to) bark	*bellen*	(to) bleed	*bluten*
base	*Basis, Sockel*	(to) bless	*segnen*
battle	*Schlacht*	bloodshed	*Blutvergießen*
bay	*(Meeres-)Bucht*	(to) blush	*erröten, rot werden*
(to) bear	*tragen*	(to) boast	*angeben, prahlen, sich rühmen*
beef	*Rindfleisch*	(to) boil	*kochen, abkochen*
(to) behave	*sich benehmen*	boot	*Kofferraum (Auto); Stiefel*
behaviour	*Verhalten, Benehmen*	border	*Grenze*
behind	*hinten, dahinter, zurück*	(to) borrow	*borgen, ausleihen*
belief	*Glaube, Überzeugung*	bottom	*Grund, unterster Teil, Boden*
(to) believe in	*glauben an*	bough [aʊ]	*Ast, Zweig*
belongings	*Habseligkeiten*	boundary	*Grenze*
below	*unten, unter*	(to) bow [aʊ]	*beugen, neigen*
belt	*Gürtel*	bow [əʊ]	*(Pfeil und) Bogen*
bench	*(Park-, Garten-)Bank*	bowl	*Schale, Schüssel, Napf*
(to) bend down	*sich bücken*	brain	*Gehirn, Verstand, Intelligenz*
benefit	*Nutzen, Vorteil*	branch	*Ast (eines Baumes); Zweigstelle*
beside	*neben*	brave	*tapfer*
besides	*außer*	breadth	*Breite, Weite*
(to) betray	*verraten*	breath	*Atem*
beyond	*jenseits, darüber hinaus*	(to) breathe	*atmen*
bill	*Rechnung*	(to) breed	*aufziehen, züchten*
bite	*Bissen, Happen*	brick	*Ziegel*
(to) blame	*die Schuld geben*	brief	*kurz, bündig*
blank	*leer, unausgefüllt, unbeschrieben*	bright	*hell*
blanket	*Decke, Wolldecke*		

vocabulary	dt. Bedeutung
(to) bring up	aufziehen, großziehen
(to) broadcast	senden, übertragen (TV)
bucket	Eimer, Kübel
burden	Last
burial	Begräbnis
(to) burn	brennen, verbrennen
(to) burst	brechen
(to) bury	begraben
business	Geschäft
button	Knopf
by birth	von Geburt
by mistake	aus Versehen
by trade	von Beruf
by virtue of	kraft [Gen.], aufgrund
campaign	Feldzug, Wahlkampf
capability	Fähigkeit
capacity	Fassungsvermögen, Aufnahmefähigkeit
capital	Hauptstadt
care	Sorgfalt
career	Karriere, Laufbahn
carpenter	Zimmerer/Zimmerin
carpet	Teppich
carriage	Wagen, (Zug-)Waggon
cash	Bargeld
(to) cast	werfen
cattle	Vieh

vocabulary	dt. Bedeutung
cause	Grund, Anlass
(to) cease	aufhören
centre	Mitte, Zentrum
century	Jahrhundert
certain	gewiss
chain	Kette
challenge	Herausforderung
(to) change	ändern
(to) charge	(Geld) verlangen; angreifen
charity	Wohltätigkeit; Güte, Nachsicht
(to) chat	schwätzen
(to) cheat	betrügen, schummeln
(to) check	kontrollieren
cheek	Backe, Wange
(to) cheer	anfeuern
chief	oberster, wichtigster, Haupt-
childhood	Kindheit
chill	Frost, Kälte
choice	(Aus-)Wahl
circumstances	Umstände, Verhältnisse
citizen	(Staats-)Bürger*in
(to) claim	behaupten; Anspruch erheben auf
clerk	Angestellte*r
(to) combine	verbinden

vocabulary	dt. Bedeutung
(to) come to terms	sich einigen, sich arrangieren
comfort	Trost
commerce	Handel
common sense	gesunder Menschenverstand
company	Gesellschaft
(to) compare	vergleichen
(to) compete	konkurrieren
(to) complain	sich beschweren
(to) complete	vervollständigen
(to) conceive	begreifen
(to) confess	gestehen, beichten
confidence	Vertrauen
(to) confirm	bestätigen, bekräftigen
(to) confuse	verwirren
(to) connect	verbinden
conscience	Gewissen
conscientious	gewissenhaft
conscious	bewusst
(to) consider	betrachten, erwägen
(to) consist of	bestehen aus
(to) consult	um Rat fragen
(to) consume	verbrauchen
(to) contain	enthalten
(to) continue	fortfahren, weitermachen
convenient	bequem, günstig
conversation	Gespräch
(to) convey	befördern, transportieren, übermitteln
(to) convince	überzeugen
(to) cough	husten
counter	Ladentisch, Theke, Schalter
courage	Mut
court	Gericht
crack	Riss, Spalte
(to) create	(er-)schaffen
crime	Verbrechen
critic	Kritiker*in
criticism	Kritik
cruel	grausam
cupboard	Schrank
curious	neugierig
current	gegenwärtig, aktuell
curse	Fluch
custom	Sitte, Brauch
damage	Schaden
damp	feucht
danger	Gefahr
(to) dare	wagen
(to) dawn	dämmern, tagen
deadline	Deadline, Frist
deaf	taub
(to) deal	austeilen, handeln
debt	Schulden

vocabulary	dt. Bedeutung	vocabulary	dt. Bedeutung
(to) decay	verfallen	(to) deserve	(eine Belohnung) verdienen
(to) deceive	täuschen	desire	Wunsch, Verlangen
(to) decide	entscheiden	(to) despair	verzweifeln
decision	Entscheidung	desperate	verzweifelt
declaration	(öffentliche) Erklärung	(to) despise	verachten
(to) declare	(öffentlich) erklären	(to) destroy	zerstören
decline	Abnahme, Niedergang, Verfall	determination	Entschlossenheit
deed	Tat, Heldentat	(to) determine	bestimmen
defeat	Niederlage	(to) develop	(sich) entwickeln
defence	Verteidigung	device	Gerät, Vorrichtung
(to) defend	verteidigen	(to) devote	widmen
(to) defy	trotzen	dictionary	Wörterbuch
degree	Grad	(to) differ	sich unterscheiden
delay	Verspätung	(to) dig	graben
deliberate	wohl überlegt, vorsätzlich	dignity	Würde
delicate	zart, zerbrechlich	(to) diminish	vermindern
delight	Vergnügen	(to) direct	richten
(to) deliver	liefern; (eine Rede) halten	disadvantage	Nachteil
demand	Nachfrage	(to) disappoint	enttäuschen
(to) deny	abstreiten, leugnen; verweigern	(to) discover	entdecken
(to) depart	abfahren	disease	Krankheit
(to) depend on/upon	abhängen von	(to) disgust	empören, entrüsten
		dishes	Geschirr
		(to) dismiss	entlassen
		(to) dissolve	auflösen
depth	Tiefe	distance	Entfernung
description	Beschreibung	(to) distinguish	unterscheiden

vocabulary	dt. Bedeutung	vocabulary	dt. Bedeutung
distinguished	*ausgezeichnet, berühmt*	effect	*Wirkung*
		efficiency	*Tüchtigkeit*
distress	*Elend, Not*	effort	*Anstrengung*
(to) distribute	*verteilen*	election	*Wahl*
(to) disturb	*stören*	electricity	*Elektrizität*
(to) divide	*teilen*	(to) employ	*beschäftigen, anstellen*
domestic	*inländisch, einheimisch*		
(to) double	*verdoppeln*	(to) enclose	*(einem Brief) beilegen*
(to) doubt	*(be-)zweifeln*	(to) encourage	*ermutigen*
drain	*Abfluss; (fig.) Abwanderung*	enemy	*Feind*in*
		engaged	*belegt, besetzt; verlobt*
draught	*Luftzug, (Durch-)Zug*		
(to) draw	*(Schlussfolgerungen) ziehen; zeichnen*	engine	*Motor*
		(to) entertain	*unterhalten*
drop	*Fall, Sturz*	entire	*ganz*
(to) drown	*ertrinken; ertränken*	entrance	*Eingang*
due to	*aufgrund, infolge*	equal	*gleich*
dust	*Staub*	equality	*Gleichheit*
duty	*Pflicht*	(to) escape	*entfliehen*
eager	*begierig*	essential	*wesentlich, notwendig*
(to) earn	*(Geld) verdienen*	established	*gegründet*
economic	*wirtschaftlich*	even	*sogar*
economical	*sparsam, wirtschaftlich*	event	*Ereignis*
		evil	*übel, böse*
edge	*Rand, Kante*	exact	*genau*
		(to) examine	*untersuchen*
(to) edit	*(Text) herausgeben, redigieren*	except	*außer*
		exception	*Ausnahme*
education	*Ausbildung*	(to) exchange	*tauschen*

vocabulary	dt. Bedeutung
existence	*Dasein, Leben, Existenz*
expense	*Kosten*
experience	*Erfahrung*
experiment	*Versuch, Experiment*
(to) explain	*erklären*
explanation	*Erklärung*
(to) explore	*erforschen*
(to) extend	*verlängern*
extension	*Ausdehnung, Verlängerung*
extent	*Ausmaß, Umfang*
fact	*Tatsache*
factory	*Fabrik*
(to) fail	*scheitern; (bei einer Prüfung) durchfallen*
failure	*Misserfolg, Versagen*
faint	*schwach*
faith	*Glaube*
faithful	*treu*
false	*falsch*
familiar	*vertraut*
fare	*Fahrgeld*
fashion	*Mode*
fast	*schnell*
(to) fasten	*festmachen*
fate	*Schicksal*
fault	*Fehler*
favour	*Gefälligkeit*

vocabulary	dt. Bedeutung
favourable	*günstig*
favourite	*Lieblings-*
fear	*Angst*
feather	*Feder*
fence	*Zaun*
fertile	*fruchtbar*
fever	*Fieber*
final	*endgültig*
finally	*schließlich*
fine	*Geldstrafe*
firm	*Firma*
fist	*Faust*
(to) fit	*passen*
flake	*Flocke*
flat	*flach*
(to) flatter	*schmeicheln*
flavour	*Geschmack*
(to) flee	*fliehen*
(to) float	*(an der Oberfläche) schwimmen*
(to) flood	*überfluten*
flour	*Mehl*
(to) flourish	*blühen, gedeihen*
(to) fold	*falten*
for good	*endgültig*
(to) forbid	*verbieten*
force	*Gewalt*
forehead	*Stirn*

vocabulary	dt. Bedeutung	vocabulary	dt. Bedeutung
foreign	*ausländisch*	giant	*riesig*
fork	*Gabel*	gift	*Geschenk; Gabe*
former	*früher, ehemalig*	(to) give a hand	*behilflich sein*
fortunate	*glücklich*	(to) give up	*aufgeben, aufhören*
fortune	*Vermögen*	glad	*froh*
frame	*Rahmen*	glasses [Pl.]	*Brille*
free of charge	*kostenlos*	glorious	*glorreich, prächtig*
(to) freeze	*(er-)frieren, gefrieren, erstarren*	glory	*Ruhm*
		glove	*Handschuh*
frequently	*oft*	good-bye	*Auf Wiedersehen, Lebewohl!*
frontier	*Grenzland, Grenze*		
(to) fry	*braten*	goods	*Waren*
fun	*Spaß*	(to) govern	*regieren*
furniture	*Möbel*	government	*Regierung*
fury	*Wut, Zorn*	gradually	*allmählich*
(to) gain	*gewinnen, profitieren*	grain	*Getreide, (Samen-)Korn*
game	*Spiel*		
gas [AE]	*Benzin*	grateful	*dankbar*
gate	*Tor, Sperre; Flugsteig*	grave	*Grab*
(to) gather	*sich versammeln*	greeting	*Begrüßung, Gruß*
gay	*homosexuell; lustig, vergnügt*	grief	*Kummer, Trauer*
		(to) grow	*wachsen*
general	*allgemein*	growth	*Wachstum*
generally	*im Allgemeinen*	(to) guard	*bewachen*
generous	*großzügig*	(to) guess	*(er-)raten; vermuten*
gentle	*sanft, leicht*	guest	*Gast*
(to) get rid of	*loswerden*	guilt	*Schuld*
(to) get up	*aufstehen*	habit	*Gewohnheit, Angewohnheit*
(to) get used to	*sich gewöhnen an*		

vocabulary	dt. Bedeutung	vocabulary	dt. Bedeutung
half	*halb; Hälfte*	husband	*(Ehe-)Mann*
hall	*Diele*	idea	*Vorstellung*
ham	*Schinken*	ideal	*vorbildlich, ideal*
(to) handle	*handhaben, behandeln*	(to) imagine	*sich vorstellen*
handsome	*gutaussehend, hübsch*	immediate	*unmittelbar, sofort*
(to) happen	*sich ereignen*	importance	*Wichtigkeit*
harbour	*Hafen*	impossible	*unmöglich*
hardly	*kaum*	impression	*Eindruck*
harm	*Schaden*	(to) improve	*verbessern*
harvest	*Ernte*	improvement	*Verbesserung*
haste	*Eile*	(to) include	*einschließen, enthalten*
hate	*Hass*	(to) increase	*zunehmen*
health	*Gesundheit*	indeed	*in der Tat, gewiss*
heap	*Haufen*	independent	*unabhängig*
heat	*Hitze*	inferior	*untergeordnet, minderwertig*
(to) hide	*verbergen*	influence	*Einfluss*
(to) hire	*mieten*	(to) inform	*benachrichtigen*
history	*Geschichte*	(to) inquire	*sich erkundigen*
hole	*Loch*	inquiry	*Anfrage; offizielle Untersuchung*
hollow	*hohl*	inside	*drinnen*
holy	*heilig*	(to) insist on	*auf etw. bestehen*
honest	*ehrlich*	instead	*stattdessen*
honour	*Ehre*	instruction	*Anweisung, Gebrauchsanweisung*
however	*jedoch*		
human	*menschlich*	(to) intend	*beabsichtigen*
(to) hunt	*jagen*	intention	*Absicht*
(to) hurry	*sich beeilen*		

vocabulary	dt. Bedeutung
interest	*Interesse; Zins*
(to) interrupt	*unterbrechen*
(to) introduce	*(jdn., sich) vorstellen*
(to) invent	*erfinden*
invention	*Erfindung*
invitation	*Einladung*
(to) invite	*einladen*
iron	*Eisen*
irregular	*ungleichmäßig, uneben*
island	*Insel*
issue	*Streitfrage*
jam	*Marmelade*
jealous	*eifersüchtig*
jealousy	*Eifersucht*
jewel	*Edelstein*
job	*Stellung, Arbeitsstelle*
(to) join	*sich anschließen, beitreten*
joke	*Witz*
journey	*Reise*
judge	*Richter*in*
judgement	*(Gerichts-)Urteil; Beurteilung, Urteil*
juice	*Saft*
justice	*Gerechtigkeit*
(to) justify	*rechtfertigen*
(to) kick	*treten*

vocabulary	dt. Bedeutung
kind	*freundlich, liebenswürdig*
kindness	*Freundlichkeit, Liebenswürdigkeit*
kingdom	*Königreich*
knife	*Messer*
knot	*Knoten*
knowledge	*Kenntnisse, Wissen*
labour	*Arbeit*
lack	*Mangel*
ladder	*Leiter*
lake	*(Binnen-)See*
lame	*lahm*
language	*Sprache*
late	*spät*
laughter	*Gelächter*
(to) lay	*legen; (Tisch) decken*
leaf	*Blatt*
(to) lend	*etw. verleihen*
length	*Länge*
level	*Höhe, Niveau*
library	*Bücherei*
(to) limit	*begrenzen*
liquid	*Flüssigkeit*
local	*örtlich*
lock	*(Tür-)Schloss*
loose	*locker*
(to) lose	*verlieren*
loss	*Verlust*

vocabulary	dt. Bedeutung	vocabulary	dt. Bedeutung
low	*niedrig; leise (Stimme)*	model	*Modell*
lungs [Pl.]	*Lunge*	moderate	*mäßig, gemäßigt*
mail	*Post*	modest	*bescheiden*
main	*Haupt-*	movement	*Bewegung*
management	*(Geschäfts-)Führung; Verwaltung*	mud	*Schlamm*
		murder	*Mord*
manager	*Leiter*in, Direktor*in*	muscle	*Muskel*
manners	*Manieren*	mysterious	*geheimnisvoll*
marks	*(Schul-)Noten*	mystery	*Geheimnis, Rätsel*
marriage	*Heirat, Ehe*	narrow	*eng, schmal*
(to) match	*(zusammen-)passen*	native	*einheimisch; (Ur-)Einwohner*in*
meadow	*Wiese*		
meaning	*Sinn, Bedeutung*	necessity	*Notwendigkeit*
means [Pl.]	*Mittel*	need	*Bedürfnis, Bedarf*
measure	*Maß, Maßnahme*	(to) neglect	*vernachlässigen*
mechanic	*Mechaniker*in*	neighbourhood	*Nachbarschaft*
(to) melt	*schmelzen*	neither	*keine*r, *s*
memory	*Gedächtnis*	nephew	*Neffe*
(to) mention	*erwähnen*	news [Pl.]	*Nachricht*
merchant	*Kaufmann/Kauffrau*	niece	*Nichte*
mercy	*Gnade, Mitleid*	noble	*edel, großzügig*
mere	*bloß*	nor	*auch nicht*
merely	*nur, bloß*	not yet	*noch nicht*
message	*Nachricht, Botschaft*	(to) note	*beachten*
mind	*Sinn, Verstand*	nowadays	*heutzutage*
mine	*Bergwerk*	(to) object	*Einspruch erheben*
misery	*Elend, Not*	objection	*Einwand*
(to) miss	*verpassen*	(to) observe	*beobachten*

vocabulary	dt. Bedeutung	vocabulary	dt. Bedeutung
occasion	*Anlass*	patience	*Geduld*
occupation	*Beschäftigung*	payment	*Zahlung, Bezahlung*
(to) occupy	*(sich) beschäftigen; besetzen*	peculiar	*eigentümlich*
offence	*Vergehen*	pencil	*Bleistift*
(to) offend	*beleidigen*	perfect	*vollkommen*
offer	*Angebot*	performance	*Vorstellung, Aufführung*
opinion	*Meinung*	permission	*Erlaubnis*
opportunity	*(günstige) Gelegenheit, Chance*	(to) persuade	*überreden*
opposite	*gegenüber*	petrol	*Benzin*
opposition	*Widerstand*	pigeon	*Taube*
order	*Auftrag*	pile	*Haufen, Stoß*
ordinary	*gewöhnlich*	pity	*Mitleid*
(to) organise	*organisieren*	plant	*Pflanze; Fabrikanlage, Werk*
origin	*Ursprung*	plate	*Teller*
otherwise	*sonst*	pleasant	*angenehm*
out of work	*arbeitslos*	pleasure	*Vergnügen*
(to) overcome	*überwinden*	poison	*Gift*
(to) owe	*schulden*	polite	*höflich*
owner	*Besitzer*in*	political	*politisch*
pain	*Schmerz*	politics	*Politik*
painful	*schmerzhaft*	popular	*beliebt*
pardon?	*wie bitte?*	population	*Bevölkerung*
particularly	*besonders*	position	*Stellung, Lage*
party	*Partei*	(to) possess	*besitzen*
(to) pass by	*vorbeigehen (an)*	possession	*Besitz*
passenger	*Reisende*r, Fahrgast*	possibility	*Möglichkeit*
past	*vorüber, vorbei*	(to) post	*auf die Post geben*

vocabulary	dt. Bedeutung	vocabulary	dt. Bedeutung
pot	Kanne	public	öffentlich
(to) present	überreichen, schenken	(to) punish	bestrafen
pressure	Druck	punishment	Strafe
(to) pretend	vorgeben, so tun als ob	purpose	Absicht, Zweck
(to) prevent from	abhalten von, hindern an	puzzle	(Kreuzwort-)Rätsel
		quantity	Menge
price	(zu bezahlender) Preis	quarrel	Streit
pride	Stolz	quite	ganz, ziemlich
prison	Gefängnis	(to) raise	(Frage) aufwerfen; (Stimme) erheben
prize	(Sieges-)Preis		
probable	wahrscheinlich	range	Auswahl
profession	(akademischer) Beruf	rank	Rang
profit	Gewinn	rare	selten
progress	Fortschritt	rate	Quote, Anteil, Verhältnis
promise	Versprechen		
(to) pronounce	aussprechen	rather	lieber
pronunciation	Aussprache	raw	roh
proof	Beweis	reason	Grund, Anlass
proper	passend, richtig, geeignet	reasonable	vernünftig
		recent	jüngst, neu
property	Eigentum, Grundstück	(to) recommend	empfehlen
		(to) recover	wiedererlangen; sich erholen
proposal	Vorschlag		
(to) propose	vorschlagen	(to) reduce	herabsetzen, verringern
(to) protect	(be-)schützen		
protein	Eiweiß, Protein	(to) refer to	sich beziehen auf
proud	stolz	reference	Bezug; Betreff
(to) prove	beweisen	(to) refuse	abschlagen, sich weigern
(to) provide	zur Verfügung stellen		
		(to) regret	bedauern

Grundwortschatz 179

vocabulary	dt. Bedeutung	vocabulary	dt. Bedeutung
regular	*regelmäßig*	rude	*unhöflich*
relation	*Beziehung*	sacrifice	*Opfer*
relative	*Verwandte*r*	safety	*Sicherheit*
relief	*Erleichterung, Hilfe*	salary	*Gehalt (Geld)*
remarkable	*bemerkenswert*	satisfactory	*zufriedenstellend*
(to) remember	*sich erinnern*	(to) satisfy	*zufriedenstellen*
(to) remind	*erinnern (an)*	(to) save	*retten; aufbewahren*
(to) remove	*beseitigen, entfernen*	savings	*Ersparnisse*
(to) repeat	*wiederholen*	scale	*Maßstab*
(to) replace	*ersetzen*	scarce	*knapp*
(to) reply	*antworten*	science	*(Natur-)Wissenschaft*
report	*Bericht*	scientist	*Wissenschaftler*in*
representative	*Vertreter*in*	scissors [Pl.]	*Schere*
request	*Bitte, Wunsch*	screen	*Bildschirm*
(to) require	*verlangen, erfordern*	search	*Suche, Nachforschung*
requirement	*Voraussetzung, Anforderung*	season	*Jahreszeit*
(to) resign	*zurücktreten*	secret	*Geheimnis*
(to) resist	*widerstehen*	secretary	*Sekretär*in*
resistance	*Widerstand*	seed	*Saat, Same*
respect	*Achtung, Respekt; Hinsicht*	sense	*Sinn, Verstand*
responsible	*verantwortlich*	sentence	*Urteil(-sspruch); Satz*
(to) retire	*in Rente gehen*	separate	*getrennt, abgesondert*
review	*Kritik*	serious	*ernst(-haft)*
reward	*Belohnung*	service	*Bedienung; Dienst*
roots	*Wurzeln*	(to) settle	*sich niederlassen; besiedeln*
rope	*Seil, Tau*	settlement	*Siedlung, Niederlassung*
rough	*rau, grob*	severe	*streng, hart*

vocabulary	dt. Bedeutung	vocabulary	dt. Bedeutung
shade	Schatten	(to) spoil	verderben, verschandeln
shame	Schande; Schamgefühl	(to) spread	ausbreiten, verteilen
shape	Form, Gestalt	square	öffentlicher Platz; Viereck
shelter	Schutz		
shore	Küste, Ufer	staff	Personal
shower	Dusche	statement	Aussage
shy	schüchtern	steady	stetig, fest, standhaft
sight	Anblick	steam	Dampf
sincere	aufrichtig	stiff	steif
single	einzeln; ledig	(to) stir	umrühren; (sich) rühren, sich regen
size	Größe		
skilful	geschickt, gewandt	stomach [k]	Magen
(to) slip	ausrutschen	straight	gerade
smell	Geruch	strength	Kraft, Stärke
smooth	glatt	(to) stretch	sich erstrecken
snake	Schlange	strict	streng
society	Gesellschaft	strike	Streik
soil	Erdboden	struggle	Kampf
(to) solve	lösen; auflösen	study	Studie
sore	wund	stupid	dumm
sorrow	Kummer, Schmerz	subject	Thema, Gegenstand
soup	Suppe	(to) succeed	Erfolg haben
sour	sauer	(to) suffer from	leiden an
source	Quelle	(to) suggest	vorschlagen
speech	Rede	suggestion	Anregung, Vorschlag
(to) spell	buchstabieren	(to) suit	passen
(to) split	teilen, spalten; (sich) trennen	supply	Angebot, Vorrat
		(to) supply	liefern

Grundwortschatz

vocabulary	dt. Bedeutung	vocabulary	dt. Bedeutung
(to) support	unterstützen	tip	Spitze; Trinkgeld
(to) suppose	annehmen, vermuten	toe	Zehe
surface	Oberfläche	tongue	Zunge
surprise	Überraschung	tool	Werkzeug
(to) swallow	schlucken	tough	zäh
(to) swear	schwören	towel	Handtuch
(to) sweat [e]	schwitzen	trace	Spur
switch	Schalter	treasure	Schatz
sympathy	Mitgefühl, Mitleid	(to) treat	behandeln
task	Aufgabe	treatment	Behandlung
(to) taste	schmecken	trial	Prozess, Verhandlung; Probe
tax	Steuer		
(to) tear	zerreißen, zerren	(to) trust	vertrauen
tendency	Tendenz, Neigung	tube	Röhre; Londoner U-Bahn
tender	zart		
tent	Zelt	ugly	hässlich
term	Bedingung; Semester	umbrella	Regenschirm
than	als (nach Komparativ)	unable	unfähig
thirsty	durstig	unemployed	arbeitslos
thorough	gründlich	unfavourable	ungünstig
thought	Gedanke	unhealthy	ungesund
thread	Faden	union	Vereinigung; Gewerkschaft
(to) threaten	bedrohen		
throat	Hals, Kehle	(to) unite	(sich) vereinigen
(to) throw	werfen	unknown	unbekannt
thus	so, auf diese Weise; folglich, somit	unless	wenn nicht
		(to) urge	drängen, dringend bitten
tight	eng; dicht	urgent	dringend

vocabulary	dt. Bedeutung	vocabulary	dt. Bedeutung
(to) use	verwenden, nutzen	whereas	wohingegen, während
useful	nützlich	whether	ob
useless	nutzlos	(to) whisper	flüstern
usual	gewöhnlich	whistle	Pfeife; Pfiff
vain	eitel	whole	ganz
valley	Tal	wholly	gänzlich
valuable	wertvoll	wide	breit
value	Wert	wide awake	hellwach
variety	Vielfalt; Sorte	widower	Witwer
vegetables [Pl.]	Gemüse	wing	Flügel
verse	Strophe	(to) wipe	(ab-)wischen, (ab-)trocknen
victory	Sieg	wire	Draht
view	Aussicht	wisdom	Weisheit
violent	gewalttätig; heftig	within	drinnen, im Innern, innerhalb
virtue	Tugend	witness	Zeuge/Zeugin
(to) visit	besuchen	(to) wonder	sich fragen; sich wundern über
(to) vote	abstimmen; wählen	(to) worry	sich sorgen
voyage	Schiffsreise	worse	schlechter, schlimmer
wage	Lohn	worst	schlechteste*r, *s
want	Mangel; Bedürfnis	worth	wert (sein)
waste	Abfall	wound	Wunde
(to) waste	verschwenden	(to) wrap	einpacken, einwickeln
weak	schwach	wrong	falsch; Unrecht
wealthy	wohlhabend, reich	youth	Jugend
weapon	Waffe	zero	Null
weight	Gewicht		
wet	nass		
wheat	Weizen